MOOCS AND LIBRARIES

Presented to

Clear Lake City - County Freeman Branch Library

By

Friends of the Freeman Library

Harris County
Public Library

your pathway to knowledge

Library Technology Essentials

About the Series

The **Library Technology Essentials** series helps librarians utilize today's hottest new technologies as well as ready themselves for tomorrow's. The series features titles that cover the A–Z of how to leverage the latest and most cutting-edge technologies and trends to deliver new library services.

Today's forward-thinking libraries are responding to changes in information consumption, new technological advancements, and growing user expectations by devising groundbreaking ways to remain relevant in a rapidly changing digital world. This collection of primers guides libraries along the path to innovation through step-by-step instruction. Written by the field's top experts, these handbooks serve as the ultimate gateway to the newest and most promising emerging technology trends. Filled with practical advice and projects for libraries to implement right now, these books inspire readers to start leveraging these new techniques and tools today.

About the Series Editor

Ellyssa Kroski is the Director of Information Technology at the New York Law Institute as well as an award-winning editor and author of 22 books including *Law Librarianship in the Digital Age* for which she won the AALL's 2014 Joseph L. Andrews Legal Literature Award. Her ten-book technology series, The Tech Set, won the ALA's Best Book in Library Literature Award in 2011. She is a librarian, an adjunct faculty member at Pratt Institute, and an international conference speaker. She speaks at several conferences a year, mainly about new tech trends, digital strategy, and libraries.

Titles in the Series

MOOCS AND LIBRARIES

Kyle K. Courtney

ROWMAN & LITTLEFIELD
Lanham • Boulder • New York • London

Published by Rowman & Littlefield
A wholly owned subsidary of The Rowman & Littlefield Publishing Group, Inc.
4501 Forbes Boulevard, Suite 200, Lanham, Maryland 20706
www.rowman.com

Unit A, Whitacre Mews, 26-34 Stannary Street, London SE11 4AB

British Library Cataloguing in Publication Information Available

Library of Congress Cataloging-in-Publication Data

Courtney, Kyle K., 1976–
MOOCs and libraries / Kyle K. Courtney.
pages cm. – (Library technology essentials ; 2)
Includes bibliographical references and index.
ISBN 978-1-4422-5293-6 (cloth : alk. paper) – ISBN 978-1-4422-5294-3 (pbk. : alk. paper) – ISBN 978-1-4422-5295-0 (ebook)
1. MOOCs (Web-based instruction)–Library applications. 2. Library orientation–Web-based instruction. 3. Library employees–In-service training–Web-based instruction. 4. Libraries and distance education. I. Title.
Z674.75.W67C67 2015
025.5'602854678–dc23
2015011493

♾ ™ The paper used in this publication meets the minimum requirements of American National Standard for Information Sciences Permanence of Paper for Printed Library Materials, ANSI/NISO Z39.48-1992.

Printed in the United States of America

To Sheila: thank you for all of your love and support.

CONTENTS

SERIES EDITOR'S FOREWORD

MOOCs and Libraries is a comprehensive guide to how to create highly effective massive open online courses (MOOCs) for your library from video lectures, tutorials, and screencasts for bibliographic instruction to staff training courses and more. MOOC guru Kyle Courtney takes you by the hand and walks you through how to do everything from planning and funding your MOOC to scripting and storyboarding your videos and even how to choose a great location for shooting. This book is jam-packed with advice and project ideas such as the ins and outs of copyright law with regard to MOOCs, how libraries are leveraging this new teaching technique, and even how to choose a video camera, microphone, and lighting kits. Each project discussed reflects the fact that this outstanding book was written specifically with the librarian in mind.

The idea for the Library Technology Essentials book series came about because there have been many drastic changes in information consumption, new technological advancements, and growing user expectations over the past few years to which forward-thinking libraries are responding by devising groundbreaking ways to remain relevant in a rapidly changing digital world. I saw a need for a practical set of guidebooks that libraries could use to inform themselves about how to stay on the cutting edge by implementing new programs, services, and technologies to match their patrons' expectations.

Libraries today are embracing new and emerging technologies, transforming themselves into community hubs and places of cocreation through makerspaces, developing information commons spaces, and even taking on new roles and formats, all the while searching for ways to decrease budget lines, add value, and prove the ROI (return on invest-ment) of the library. The Library Technology Essentials series is a col-lection of primers to guide libraries along the path to innovation through step-by-step instruction. Written by the field's top experts, these handbooks are meant to serve as the ultimate gateway to the newest and most promising emerging technology trends. Filled with practical advice and project ideas for libraries to implement right now, these books will hopefully inspire readers to start leveraging these new techniques and tools today.

Each book follows the same format and outline, guiding the reader through the A–Z of how to leverage the latest and most cutting-edge technologies and trends to deliver new library services. The "Projects" chapters comprise the largest portion of the books, providing library initiatives that can be implemented by both beginner and advanced readers accommodating for all audiences and levels of technical exper-tise. These projects and programs range from the basic "How to Circu-late Wearable Technology in Your Library" and "How to Host a FIRST Robotics Team at the Library" to intermediates such as "How to Create a Hands-Free Digital Exhibit Showcase with Microsoft Kinect" and the more advanced options such as "Implementing a Scalable E-Resources Management System" and "How to Gamify Library Orientation for Pa-trons with a Top Down Video Game." Readers of all skill levels will find something of interest in these books.

It's fitting that Kyle Courtney was just named a 2015 *Library Jour-nal* Mover and Shaker; he's a leading-edge trailblazer whose knowledge and experience really shine through in this book. As copyright advisor at Harvard University and HarvardX, the university's MOOC initiative, he's been writing and speaking about MOOCs and libraries for years. When I realized that the set needed a book on the topic I just knew that Kyle had to write it. If you're looking for a comprehensive book that will teach you how to create engaging, innovative MOOCs from planning to production, this is the book for you.

—Ellyssa Kroski
Director of Information Technology
New York Law Institute
http://www.ellyssakroski.com/
http://ccgclibraries.com/

ellyssakroski@yahoo.com

PREFACE

Since their inception, MOOCs (massive open online courses) have been confusingly heralded as the future of higher education but also equally disparaged as a failed experiment because of high dropout rates. Regardless of these divergent viewpoints, MOOCs, in some capacity, are here to stay. More colleges, schools, and other institutions are investing the time and resources to create MOOC experiences. This puts libraries in an excellent position to continue to promote their mission in a new medium, providing expertise, support, and information to their communities.

What has started with toe-dipping on the part of public libraries and K–12 schools into the MOOC environment will likely become a more entrenched effort as these early experiences are studied and refined. With the advance of various types of screencasting, recording, and editing technologies, libraries can more easily create, market, and share their knowledge through the unique MOOC medium. Expert knowledge is not necessary to produce high-quality MOOC videos. Libraries themselves can revisit their traditional bibliographic instruction sessions, research seminars, and community outreach programs by using the enhanced interactivity that a MOOC can provide. One size does not fit all, and even as academic institutions dominate the MOOC landscape, public libraries and K–12 can be expected to leverage the technology and scope of MOOCs to innovative ends.

The role of libraries in MOOC development, which is rooted in collaboration, is one of great potential. While MOOCs are somewhat of a moving target, they present a unique opportunity for libraries to add expertise and value both to internal stakeholders and to the global community of MOOC participants.

ORGANIZATION OF THIS BOOK

Readers will learn all about MOOC creation, from early stage planning to pedagogy, equipment selection, filming, and launch. Each chapter is designed to build upon prior chapters as you are taking through the entire phase of MOOC creation. I encourage the reader to work through the book consecutively, as it outlines the MOOC process, but chapters have been designed to be independent and readers may jump from chapter to chapter.

AUDIENCE FOR THIS BOOK

This book has been primarily written for librarians. However, anyone who wants an introduction to the nuts and bolts of MOOC development may also find it valuable.

ACKNOWLEDGMENTS

I would like to thank Ellyssa Kroski first and foremost. As series editor, she had the vision of a clairvoyant about this particular MOOC book. Having worked with Ellyssa before, I was aware of how fantastically organized and efficient she is—but for this book, her endless patience, understanding, and advice truly helped craft the book to be the best representation of my ideas. I am thankful for her guidance, effort, suggestions, and good-natured humor. It has been a pleasure working with her.

I want to thank John Swope, founder of Curricu.me. John had the early vision to compare MOOC platforms and continued to challenge my notion of what truly "makes a MOOC" in his reviews and writings. John runs his own full-service consultancy that helps organizations build enterprise-quality online courses but gladly took the time to work with me, and I am thankful for that.

Lastly, I want to thank Emily Kilcer, who works with me every day. Emily kindly offered her keen eye to draft chapters, suggested some clever edits, and was willing to listen to my concerns, which ultimately helped make the book a real reflection of my vision for MOOCs and libraries. We should all be so lucky to have such a smart and excellent coworker just down the hall.

I

AN INTRODUCTION TO MOOCS

WHAT ARE MOOCS?

A massive open online course (MOOC) is defined simply as a course of study made available over the Internet without charge to a very large number of people. MOOCs can take on just about any form of online learning, benefiting fully from the modern technological environment.

Massive

MOOCs by their very definition are typically large classes. They range from a class of five hundred participants (for example, CopyrightX hosted by edX) to a class of 160,000 participants (for example, the artificial intelligence course from Stanford University). The size of the class adds to the complexity of the interaction, and each sized class will feature different types of content, as we will see in later chapters.

Open

MOOCs vary in their degree of openness. Participants can range from students at the hosting institution's campus to anyone else in the world with Internet access. MOOCs typically offer a variety of pedagogical activities, which might include watching videos, responding on discussion boards, building a class wiki, taking online assessments, or posting on social media platforms.

Online

Again, anyone in the world with Internet access may join a MOOC. The nature of the Internet and the value of connectedness is a feature that really enhances a MOOC course of study. While classrooms may be filled with people of similar backgrounds, experiences, and general uniformity, MOOCs offer a worldwide perspective on learning and engagement.

Course

Initially MOOCs were designed similarly to classroom learning—a lecture, discussion, and assessment—just in an online environment. However, as we have seen recently, the definition of "course" can include short learning modules, self-paced classes, solo learning objects, and a host of other "course" concepts. The MOOC course is only limited by the imagination of the instructor.

HISTORY OF FREE, ONLINE EDUCATION

Correspondence Learning

The development of technology has always been a driving force in education. The origins of MOOCs reside in a rich distance-learning history that arose in three distinct phases: correspondence courses, audiovisual courses, and finally, computer/Internet-enhanced courses.

With the advent of a reliable and cheap mail system in the United States, there was a rise in correspondence course work, which allowed study at home. Students could take a class, get feedback, and still seek a higher degree, regardless of their location in the United States. This type of correspondence course was also popular in Europe and other continents. (For example, in the nineteenth century, Australian students could take correspondence courses from the London School of Economics and other colleges and universities.)

Learning with Early Media

With the influx of radio and television, yet another form of correspondence learning was launched. Now potential students who were geographically located far from any college or university could obtain educational training through the radio or television. However, this method of training suffered from a lack of feedback and assessment, a key component of the correspondence model.

With the advent of the VCR, a hybrid audiovideo correspondence model evolved. Students could watch video tapes of lectures received in the mail and complete the assignments (quizzes or term papers) necessary for feedback and assessment. All that was required was a VCR and a television.

In 1969, the United Kingdom launched the Open University, building upon the hybrid correspondence model. Open University provided residential short courses and support services at local and regional levels, combined with correspondence assessment and public television broadcasting.

Early MOOCs

Before the term MOOC was coined, there were a number of efforts early on that harnessed the power of the Internet and connected networks to share learning globally. Using basic tools on his home computer, Salman Khan began making short math-tutoring videos, first for his younger cousins, then for anyone following his YouTube account, and eventually for millions of students around the world. That has grown into Khan Academy, a nonprofit provider of video lectures and exercises on a variety of subjects, and now, although Khan isn't a formally trained educator, he is one of the best-known teachers in the world.

Another early MOOC-like effort was iTunes U, launched by Apple in 2007, to offer educational materials for download. Many colleges and universities joined the service, creating courses specifically designed for the iTunes format or simply posting podcasts, video lectures, or textbooks for free download by anyone in the world.

Lastly, MIT started a project called OpenCourseWare (OCW). The goal of OCW was to make all of MIT's course materials available online for free. It features a variety of videos, lecture notes, texts, and other articles for use in classrooms at MIT. Users of this site can adopt the materials for use in their classes, or take a self-paced course themselves using the materials from the classroom.

MOOCs Entrance

The first class to use the acronym "MOOC" was launched in 2008 and titled "Connectivism and Connective Knowledge/2008 (CCK08)," by Stephen Downes and George Siemens. Adapted from the University of Manitoba class, this MOOC featured a variety of technologies and platforms to teach and engage with learners across the world—including an early MOOC use of Facebook, wikis, and discussion boards. Approximately 2,200 people signed up for the course.

Individuals involved in the early development of MOOCs as an instructional strategy included Siemens and Downes's CCK08, the University of Illinois's no-credit course with 2,700 participants in 2011, and the legendary artificial intelligence course by Sebastian Thrun and Peter Norvig (CS221) with 160,000 participants from 190 different countries. As a result of these massive numbers, Thrun launched Udacity, a for-profit company providing alternative lifelong learning options primarily in computer science and math.

In 2012, the big three MOOCs launched: Udacity, Coursera, and edX. Thrun had launched Udacity. In May 2012, Harvard and MIT launched the uniquely nonprofit edX, with numerous partners joining later. EdX's unique mission was to explore innovative ways to both offer classes online and use lessons and research to improve classroom education. Also in 2012, the for-profit company Coursera was founded by Stanford professors Daphne Koller and Andrew Ng. Coursera partners with leading universities to provide educational access to all.

In recent years, colleges have continued to host traditional classes in online formats for tuition-paying students for degree-seeking credit. As the public knows, you can earn an entire online degree from a growing number of collegiate programs. These programs are neither massive nor open like MOOCs, but they do have certain advantages when it comes to access, law, and licensing that we will discuss in a later chapter. For example, Colorado State University, Global Campus, has been open and online since 2008, and boasts over nine thousand students, at a fully accredited 100 percent online "campus."

Such programs demonstrate that online learning is clearly possible. Many of the technologies utilized in these classes were the foundation for modern MOOCs.

What Are SPOCs?

SPOC stands for a "small private online course," a type of smaller MOOC. The word was coined by Armando Fox at University of California, Berkeley, part of the edX family of institutions. At first, SPOCs were thought of as a concept by which MOOCs could be marketed to smaller schools or businesses as a revenue model. However, SPOCs have taken on a life of their own.

The smaller class size can give students more "virtual time" with the professor and fellow participants. There may be room for more assessment and potential to have coursework graded by the professor or his teaching assistants (TAs)—similar to a live classroom. For example, HarvardX's first SPOC, a law school course titled "HLS1x: CopyrightX," debuted in January 2013. It was taught by Professor William W. Fisher, III, and his teaching staff chose from 4,100 applicants worldwide to form the five-hundred-student online class. The class featured live events, discussion groups, weekly assignments, and a law school–style final exam, featuring several legal hypotheticals, which were answered by the students in essay form. The essays were graded by the teaching staff, which was comprised of law students and graduates of the copyright class.

WHERE ARE THE LIBRARIES?

We have outlined the history of MOOCs, their concepts, and their goals, but you may be wondering if there is a role for the library in the modern MOOC environment. The answer is, yes, very much so. There are multiple potential roles for libraries in MOOCs including development, support, assessment, modeling, teaching, and preservation. Many of these topics will be discussed in the later chapters, but know that truly, there is no limit to how a library can support a MOOC, depending on your organization. Some libraries are already active participants in

MOOCs, and the following chapters will outline their work, projects, successes, and challenges.

2

GETTING STARTED WITH MOOCS

MAIN FEATURES OF A MOOC

Now that we have briefly defined a massive open online course (MOOC), and some of the roles that librarians are playing inside a MOOC, what are the specific main features we should consider when starting to work with MOOCs at our libraries?

This chapter will outline some of the considerations that should be addressed up front: from price considerations to content delivery. And we will hear directly from some librarians who are on the front lines, identifying their challenges in MOOC creation and some of their solutions.

MOOC TIMING

Scheduled

Most MOOCs have, much like the classroom, traditional start dates and end dates and are accessible only during that time. Participants work on the class on their own time but not at their own pace. Some MOOCs feature deadlines for assignments or group work. Some, such as CopyrightX, even feature a final exam. For these scheduled courses, more often than not, once the MOOC ends the content is archived and inaccessible until the next offering.

Coursera and edX MOOCs work on this scheduled model. Only a portion of the classes in their catalogs are active at a given time. For a few weeks after a class starts, participants may still be able to enroll. However, assignment deadlines may have passed, making it impossible to earn a completion certificate. And even if participants are not concerned with the certificate, they may not be able to catch up and do all the work before the course ends.

One clear advantage of the scheduled model is that participants will have thousands of peers for a robust and engaging course—from work in discussion boards to group projects. Having a worldwide virtual classroom is one of the main reasons the MOOC environment is central to a truly global curriculum. Where else could you get the reflection on a reading, assignment, or research from peers from upward of one hundred different countries and cultures?

A disadvantage of the scheduled model is that potential participants may have to wait months for the course to be opened, updated, and relaunched. Occasionally, some of these classes do not meet the criteria for relaunch and are permanently retired.

Self-Paced

While many MOOCs have the day the course begins, some do not have the rigid scheduling and semester-like planning. Some MOOCs of this variety offer a self-paced model, which is always accessible. This is similar to MIT's Open Courseware model, which allows participants to start and finish on their schedule; the content will always remain online and available.

Many Udacity classes work on this self-paced scheduling. However, there is a distinct downside to self-paced MOOCs: there are typically very few opportunities to interact with other participants, the professor, or any MOOC support staff. Often discussion boards and forums will be sparsely active. Any quiz, test, or assessment would be automated at best, and there are few opportunities for curriculum updates.

MOOC CERTIFICATION

Certification or course-completion certificates are something that many MOOCs offer to participants at the end of a MOOC course. Some of these are free, and some cost money. The decision to offer these certificates should be made up front.

Free Certificates and Verified Certificates

Initially, completion of a MOOC resulted in something as simple as an e-mail of "congratulations." Later, MOOCs offered free "certificates of completion" for those participants that completed each lecture, quiz, discussion board, or other assessment. These certificates were not verifiable in any real way, which made sense, since MOOCs were not offering credits.

However, as employers, employees, and students at other universities were using MOOCs as a form of skills or resume building, major MOOC providers thought they could offer the participants something more official.

For years Udacity-based courses issued free certificates of completion. At the time, to get a certificate, a participant had to sign up and complete the online course. However, as of May 2014, Udacity decided to no longer offer free non-identity-verified certificates. They claimed their action was in response from students and employers asking for more rigor in certifying actual accomplishments. Participants may still take Udacity classes for free; however, you can't get credentials unless you go through their fee-based verification process.

Verified certificates, used also by Coursera and edX, require you to use a webcam and some form of government ID to confirm your real identity. This check is to ensure that the registered participant was also the person doing the course work toward the certificate. At the time of this writing, price ranges for the certificates go from forty to one hundred dollars, depending on the course.

Advanced Certificates

If the MOOC you are creating is part of a series of classes with a concentration or focus, both Coursera and edX offer another certificate participants can earn by completing the sequence of classes on a particular subject.

For example, if a participant completes a sequence of three courses in "The Civil War and Reconstruction" from Columbia or a series of four classes on astrophysics from Australia National University, participants can earn an advanced "XSeries" certificate. At Coursera, these advanced certificates are called "specializations" and require the completion of a series of courses, followed by a capstone project. Some of the capstone projects involve more advanced, hands-on learning projects, video conferencing with instructors, or publication of the final capstone project.

MOOC STAFFING: BUILD UPON WHAT'S ALREADY THERE

Staffing is a critical component of all projects in libraries. Whether the MOOC is run by a university, a public library, or a consortia group, staffing considerations should be assessed up front. As described in the introductory chapter, the number of roles librarians can fill in the creation and delivery of a MOOC has real-world, real-budgeting consequences. Each library should carefully asses the how and why of each potential MOOC production or support.

The good news is that you can build upon what you have in your library. Many libraries have a department, specialization, or staff dedicated to teaching, learning, outreach, or curriculum-based work. These are excellent places to start. Staff time dedicated to a MOOC not only builds great opportunities for professional development and expertise but also can aid the mission of the library itself. There is nothing to say that a research video, instructional tutorial, or other MOOC product can always be used in-house at your own library. If the staffing helps both the MOOC launch and the library mission, it may be well worth the time.

MOOC "PARTICIPANTS"

In the early days of MOOC terminology, the word "students" was used frequently. However, the word "student" carries some financial and legal definitions, especially in the education field. "Students" are typically paying customers at an academic institution and therefore can take advantage of the various privileges provided by the university—access to libraries, databases, and online networks, in particular. Additionally, the word "students" indicates mandatory compliance with various privacy laws, especially about educational data. Laws such as the Family Educational Rights and Privacy Act (FERPA) and the Higher Education Opportunity Act protect student information, and require schools, colleges, universities, and other educational institutions to take steps to comply. These laws apply even to distance-education classes, which like MOOCs, are available remotely online. However, unlike MOOCs, students pay for credits for the distance-learning classes.

In the MOOC landscape, however, no such student rights exist. MOOC "students" are not matriculated into a particular college or university simply by taking a MOOC run by that university. They do not take class for credits, pay tuition, or have access to the libraries, databases, or other privileges reserved for students. As a result they should be called "participants," which denotes the voluntary and free nature of the MOOC course, and the fact that FERPA, and other higher education student rights, do not apply to the MOOC context.

CREATING YOUR OWN MOOC

Creating your own MOOC in your library is not a simple task. There are many things to consider before starting such an ambitious project. In this section, we start to review some of the most critical factors in MOOC creation: pedagogy, copyright, the syllabus, and licensing.

MOOC Pedagogy

Many MOOCs have to balance a number of goals in the creation of a course: offering the best teaching possible in the MOOC environment; providing students the materials they need to complete the class; producing courses that can be distributed worldwide; minimizing any legal risk; and making efficient use of limited resources, both financial and human.

Most importantly, not everything that works in the face-to-face classroom will work online. Many classroom fundamentals will need to be reworked to fit the MOOC technology, and certain classroom exercises will require an entirely different approach. As a example faced by most MOOC creators, let's imagine a simple discussion activity that would be assessed in a face-to-face class. Obviously, this is not suitable to the online environment. We might have to think of a way to harness the MOOC platform, video technology, or discussion-board basics, or have a peer-to-peer grading session of short essays.

Many librarians will find that you will need to adjust your teaching style or pedagogy for this particular group of MOOC participants. But you must also have realistic expectations. While it would be ideal to have multiple video clips for each teaching point, librarians need to consider the resources required to make each video and how it will affect the participant's learning experience, and the levels of support students might need for each concept. To solve these complex pedagogical quagmires, it is best to start with a simple design and focus on the learning outcomes. Some MOOC designers look to "stepping into the shoes" of the MOOC participants—how would the average users view the video, syllabus, exercises, quizzes, and so forth? Librarians should access their MOOC course as a participant and check to see if the instructions are clear and the design and learning goals are simple enough to support a broad array of learners.

Some MOOCs have harnessed a recent educational concept called "backward design" to aid the MOOC creation. In the book *Understanding by Design*, by Grant Wiggins and Jay McTighe,[1] the authors describe a structure for designing courses that can be applied to work within any class, not just for MOOCs. Their "backward design" method begins by first identifying *what* students should learn from the material, before considering *how* the instructor might approach teaching it. The outcome of their method creates a results-oriented course plan that works very well in the early stages of MOOC design.

Let's look briefly at the first part of backward design to emphasize its usefulness to the MOOC creation process. First, librarians should establish learning goals for the MOOC: What should participants know, understand, and be able to do? And how does the instructor prioritize and narrow down the content that she or he wants to teach, so it fits within the limited framework of the MOOC? Wiggins and McTighe provide a useful process for establishing curricular priorities. They suggest instructors ask themselves three questions and focus on the most valuable content:

1. What should participants hear, read, view, explore, or otherwise encounter in the MOOC? This knowledge is "worth being familiar with."
2. What knowledge and skills should participants master? Sharpen your choices by considering what is "important to know and do" for your participants. What facts, concepts, and principles should they know? What processes, strategies, and methods should they learn to use?
3. What are the big ideas and important understandings participants should retain? These choices are the "enduring understandings" that you want participants to remember after they've forgotten the details of the MOOC.

Answering each of these questions will help you determine the best content for your course and create concrete, specific learning goals for your MOOC participants. Prepare answers to these questions, and create the MOOC learning objectives before engaging in content creation. This will make course development far more efficient, and will serve as the guide for the overall course development.

In addition, the following topics are some of the top considerations for developing a successful MOOC pedagogy. Remember, not every category needs to be addressed in the MOOC, but it is important to note how these categories will affect the participant's learning experience.

Communication and Engagement

• Instructor contact. Your frequent and ongoing presence is invaluable to student success in a MOOC. When the MOOC begins, connect with participants right away and continue a beneficial level of contact throughout the course. The participants should have a sense of the instructor's presence through the MOOC. This not only makes participants feel welcome and engaged in the course but also creates an open line of communication throughout the course.

- Casual contact. Many MOOCs aid this process with a "watercooler" and "introduce yourself" section on the discussion boards. This allows the instructor to learn about a participant's background (introduce yourself) and also strike up conversations related to the MOOC—but not necessarily about the substance of the MOOC.
- Communication assignments. Assign the discussion forum and one response as one of the first MOOC assignments. Some MOOCs make this a survey form, some create a series of questions that would make up a mini online biography, and some make it free form (with a word limit or no word limit).
- Encourage contact and cooperation among students. The exchange of ideas, opinions, arguments, perspectives, and questions is essential to a successful learning experience.
- Communicate high expectations. High expectations, with appropriate support, lead to high rates of student success.

Review and Comment Frequently

- Discussion-board responses. The more an instructor takes time and effort into the discussion-board portion of a MOOC, the more participants will do the same. The key is to budget your time in discussion boards to ensure you make your presence felt, without dominating the discussion. So, how do you do this?
- Schedule participation check-in. Instructors should schedule their check-ins to comport with the goals, assignments, and discussion in the MOOC. The more regular the check-in (one a day; twice a day; Monday, Wednesday, and Friday; etc.), the more organized and focused the discussion will be.
- Weigh your responses—do not respond to everything. Instructors do not, and should not, post a response to every comment in the discussion board. With some MOOCs participation rates in the thousands, and this wouldn't even be possible. Instructors ought to make specific comments to certain participant's posts if they are accurate, challenging, or cause a new or an interesting line of inquiry. Remember, the discussion board is supposed to mimic the in-class discussion

pedagogy, so posts that encourage deeper discussion should be built upon.

- Ask another question inside the response. Some of the best instructor responses ask the participant to research and answer again, and perhaps ask other participants to answer each other's questions. This can serve two purposes: (1) deepen the discussion that is on point, or (2) nudge the participants back on the topic if the answer is not on point.

Provide Effective Feedback

- Give prompt feedback. Feedback that is timely, constructive, and supportive increases student satisfaction and achievement.
- Written feedback. The most standard form of feedback for MOOCs is through written feedback, provided through discussion boards, writing assignments, written assessments, quizzes, tests, or other methods. If it is in a public discussion forum, remember to answer the question so that each participant can get something from the exchange. Effective written feedback will provide a lesson for the individual participant and continue to the learning process for the rest of the MOOC participants as well.
- Video feedback. Feedback in a MOOC is not just in writing; in fact, written feedback is just one simple way to provide participant feedback. Just as in the classroom, more intricate or subtle issues may require "face-to-face" feedback that MOOC technology can allow. Instructors can use your basic webcam to send recorded video feedback. Send a video summarizing the week's discussion, or send individual feedback to groups or subgroups of MOOC participants.
- Give students opportunities for reflection. New perspectives, nuanced understanding, and deeper appreciation emerge from awareness, critical analysis, and self-exploration.

Manage Time Wisely

- Instructor time. Set expectations with students with respect to instructor response times. Indicate turnaround for grading assignments, responding to e-mail, and posting to discussion boards. Outline policies for late or delayed submissions.
- Participant time. A useful early assignment for a MOOC may ask participants to describe how they will manage the MOOC work. Do

they have other jobs, responsibilities, or time off planned ahead? It may be important to allow MOOC participants to think about this, and respond, during the first few modules or lessons. One trap online students may fall prey to is to mismanage their time and attempt to complete and submit multiple assignments in batches, rather than on a well-paced schedule. You can help your students to be more successful by encouraging them to be mindful of this and to practice good online learning behaviors.

Consult with Other MOOC Specialists

- Other MOOC communities. There are a host of other people involved with MOOCs in libraries, colleges, universities, and other learning communities such as instructional designers, librarians, MOOC instructors, learning technologists, information specialists, and more. Reaching out to them, through their communities and through blogs, listservs, and articles may inspire new innovations, designs, or creations of a MOOC.

Help Your Students to Be Successful Online Learners

- In person versus MOOC. In an online environment, students must be more self-directed, manage their time efficiently, and assume greater responsibility for their own learning than they would in a more guided, hand-holding classroom environment. Consider this when creating your content, assignments, and assessments.
- Provide participant support. Do you have the time to serve as both instructor and troubleshooter? Make sure there are resources, if necessary, both financial and human, available for those questions and problems with any aspect of the MOOC course. This could be as simple as a brief video tutorial on discussion boards to a bibliography on further information resources on the MOOC topic.
- Respect different styles of learning. Many students learn in different ways. If possible, provide ways in which different learners can excel in your MOOC. Allow participants to submit a video instead of a biography. Film different MOOC segments in different locations, related to the topic, and use visual learning aids. Offer multiple-choice quizzes one week and short-answer analysis the following

week. Interpret the results, and realize a diverse body of participants in your MOOC can only enhance the learning experience.

- Pay attention to potential plagiarism and other forms of academic dishonesty. Plagiarism is a real threat to the MOOC environment. The "copy and paste" method of academic shortcuts has only increased since the birth of the Internet. However, the Internet also makes it easy to find works of academic dishonesty. Make it clear that this will not be accepted, and in the case of cultural or social difference, address your concerns immediately and supply a resolution.
- Adapt course design and syllabus for online delivery. A clear, consistent structure of course elements is essential for the online environment. You may need to change and alter your on-ground syllabus substantially. Don't make it difficult for the participant—be clear, be concise, and be helpful. Many MOOC participants have not had much experience with online education.

Copyright Law and MOOCs

Having a resource for copyright law in the library is a critical component of successful twenty-first-century libraries. The ALA lists copyright, along with some other relevant laws, as a core competency of librarianship. As librarians, we want to provide whatever our patrons desire, but we must also balance the law versus the user's needs. Fortunately, copyright law does not always restrict certain uses. In many cases a solid understanding of copyright can help ease fears, provide legal alternatives to a request, or help educate the community at large. In the MOOC context, basic knowledge of copyright law will aid any library looking to become an engaging, critical component of any MOOC process.

Current Copyright Law

The current copyright law in the United States is the Copyright Act of 1976. All of the copyright laws passed by Congress exist pursuant to article 1, section 8, clause 8, of the Constitution, which gives Congress the power "to promote the Progress of Science and useful Arts, by securing for limited Times to Authors and Inventors the exclusive Right to their respective Writings and Discoveries." This section of the Constitution is known as the "Copyright Clause."

Under the current law, the Copyright Act of 1976 ("Copyright Act"), copyright protection begins immediately at the creation of an original "work of authorship fixed in any tangible medium of expression." Under the current Copyright Act, a copyright typically lasts for the life of an individual author or authors, plus seventy years. Alternatively, if a corporation is the author, the term is 95 years from creation or 120 years from publication, whichever is sooner.

On March 1, 1989, the United States agreed to the Berne Convention of International Copyright. This eliminated the formalities of copyright registration. Authors no longer needed to put a copyright notice on their work. Additionally, it no longer required registration with the U.S. Copyright Office. However, although registration is optional, the Copyright Office offers advantages for registration. For example, registration is a prerequisite to filing a copyright infringement suit in federal court.

Instantly you can see how copyright might impact a MOOC—the more modern the image, the less likely it will be in the public domain and open to use in a MOOC. Additionally, the images MOOC faculty and staff choose may list no copyright information at all—but that does not mean it is not covered by copyright. It is just a result of eliminating the requirement for registration and notice. Drawing content from the Internet for a MOOC is ripe with copyright problems, without careful thought and risk analysis.

What Is Copyrightable?

The Copyright Act lists the following types of works of authorship as those that can be protected by copyright:

- literary works
- musical works, including any accompanying words
- dramatic works, including any accompanying music
- pantomimes and choreographic works
- pictorial, graphic, and sculptural works
- motion pictures and other audiovisual works
- sound recordings
- architectural works

Typically, these categories are viewed quite broadly. For example, since a computer program is written in computer code, it is considered a literary work. Of the hundreds of MOOCs offered since 2008, nearly *every one of these categories* of copyright has been used in a MOOC.

Rights of a Copyright Holder

Let's say you do publish an original work of authorship. What rights do you have as the owner of that work? Copyright owners have exclusive rights to

- reproduce the work (make copies);
- prepare derivative works based upon the copyrighted work;
- distribute the work;
- publically perform the work; and
- publically display the work.

There are also other specific rights enumerated for particular kinds of works.[2]

These are all considered the "bundle of rights" of the copyright owner. Any of these individual rights may be given away, licensed, sold, or any combination thereof. They are like pieces of property that can be allocated by the owner. For example, many musicians license their rights of reproduction and distribution to music distributors, so the distributer can legally make, ship, and sell CDs, MP3s, and other copies of the music. Alternatively, it is possible to transfer one right, while retaining all other rights.

If a person utilizes any of these rights without permission of the copyright owner, he or she may be liable for infringement. In the MOOC environment, we can see especially how the right to reproduce the work, distribute the work, and display or perform the work could be infringement by simply including the material in a MOOC class and uploading it to the Internet or sharing it with potentially thousands of participants. In those cases, there needs to be a determination whether the MOOC is infringing the copyright holder's rights.

Infringement

To succeed on a claim for direct infringement under the Copyright Act, a plaintiff must show the following: (1) ownership of valid copyright, and (2) unauthorized copying or violation of one of other exclusive rights afforded copyright owners pursuant to Copyright Act.

Beyond direct infringement there is the doctrine of secondary liability. This arises when one party is held legally responsible for the actions of another party. For example, in the MOOC context, although a library, staff member, or agent of a MOOC may have allegedly uploaded the infringing content, the hosting university, college, or program might be "secondarily liable" for such infringement.

However, there is an exception for libraries involved in such cases. If the infringer is a library or archive, or the employee of a library or archive, then the court can lower or eliminate damages altogether if the infringer "believed and had reasonable grounds for believing that his or her use of the copyrighted work was a fair use under § 107." Whether or not this would apply in the MOOC context is yet to be seen. But as you can imagine, it is a relevant portion of the statute, and yet another reason for libraries, which are "judgment proof" in some ways, to be involved in MOOCs. To help support this in practice, a library should try to retain any documentation that determined the alleged use was a fair use. We will learn more about fair use later.

SYLLABUS MATERIALS: LIBRARIES AND COPYRIGHT

It is a common library practice for a patron to ask a library about the very materials in the library's collection—whether in print, online, or in a database—and, naturally, they do the same when asking a copyright question about the materials in the library. This puts the library in a special position, especially when it comes to harnessing the library collections for mass distribution in a MOOC. Libraries are in the best position as the physical custodians of the works to have some knowledge about the rights related to the work.

As a preliminary matter, it is worth noting that use of third-party material in an online MOOC presents different copyright challenges than use of such material in on-campus teaching. The flexible exemption for performances and displays of copyrighted material in the course of face-to-face instruction is not available in the online context. Ideally, MOOC institutions need to take copyright issues into account from the start in designing and developing a course.

MOOCs often employ third-party copyrighted materials in the online videos. This will include text, graphs, figures, images, maps, video clips, music recordings, and other works of authorship that appear in the presentation. Many librarians will have to have knowledge of copyright and fair use if they are to support a MOOC in this way. Suffice it to say that typically, there must be a reasonable fair-use basis for any third-party copyrighted material included in an instructional presentation without the copyright holder's permission. We will talk about fair-use policies developed at libraries later in the book.

However, the present state of affairs with copyright and educational materials requires that there should be a basic distinction between the two kinds of materials used in a MOOC course:

- "Presentation materials," that is, materials used by the instructor in a presentation to students (for example, in a slides accompanying a lecture); and
- "Syllabus materials," that is, materials provided to students for their independent use in conjunction with the course (for example, assigned textbooks or articles).

Because the copyright analysis for these two kinds of materials differs in important ways, each library should adopt a separate approach for each. As illustrated later, in the sample policy from a Coursera University of Pennsylvania course guide, the approach for presentation materials involves both permissions and fair use. The approach for syllabus materials will typically rely on directing students to copies of the material lawfully available online or elsewhere, including open-access materials. (See chapter 4 for a case study of HarvardX's syllabus material policies.)

It should be emphasized that the absolute safest way to avoid infringement is to use material that is of the MOOC's own creation (created by the library, the instructor, or the institution launching the MOOC), that is in the public domain, or that is available under general license terms that permit this activity, such as certain Creative Commons licenses. The second safest way is to seek permission.

LICENSING AND PERMISSION

Many MOOC instructors understand that, traditionally, when a journal accepts an article for publication, the publisher sends the author a publication agreement to sign and return. This agreement usually requires the author to assign the copyright to the publisher, with the author occasionally retaining limited rights.

It may not be a surprise to hear that many faculty members, librarians, and other authors were not clear on how that agreement might impact their use of their authored textbooks and articles for their MOOC classes. For example, faculty members want to use their authored articles or book for class. Surprise! You have *no rights* to share this article per your publication agreement, and especially cannot share with the potential thousands of students that make up a MOOC course. Again, this level of distribution would be tantamount to serious contract breaches or copyright infringement.

However, this gives the library a great opportunity to talk with the faculty about publication agreements, open access, and institutional repositories. At Harvard, which has a university-wide Open Access Policy, faculty authors in participating schools grant the university a nonexclusive, irrevocable right to distribute their scholarly articles for any noncommercial purpose. Scholarly articles provided to the university are stored, preserved, and made freely accessible in digital form in DASH, Harvard University Library's open-access repository. Many faculty members learned how their works could be located in DASH and that this would be a great access point to provide links to the MOOC students. Additionally, some faculty members explored other open repositories (subject specific or other institutions) with the express purpose of finding syllabus materials that matched their pedagogical aims that were also open and freely linkable. This helped avoid the "permission two-step," a syllabus policy outlined in chapter 4.

However, many faculty members still felt they needed to use a specific article that was previously licensed to the publisher. At some libraries, there is a very small team that will request, or guide the faculty and staff in requesting, a free permission from the rights-holder for use in a MOOC course. However, seeking this free permission may substantially limit the material they can acquire. Permission will likely come with some conditions and restrictions (for example, it may cover only a single semester), and there must be plenty of time for the permissions process. Lastly, the faculty should prepare to adjust readings as necessary if permission is not granted.

Many publishers are wary of granting permission, much less free permission. In the beginning of the MOOC movement, some publishers had never even heard of MOOCs at all. While that has changed, and many publishers are aware of MOOCs, the responses still vary. For example, there was a negotiation for a chapter from an Internet protocol (IP) law and economics book published by a large company (across the Atlantic), to be used in an edX MOOC course. They asked for $3,500 for permission to use the chapter. The chapter was a total of seventeen pages from a book published in 2001. The course team replied that this was a nonprofit, educational, free course, and they had requested free permission. The published responded with a lower $1,800 offer. Again, it would have cost them nothing to give permission and might have even driven up the sale and interest in the book, which was printed over a decade ago. The edX faculty member, who had published with them before, and reviewed numerous articles, wrote to them asking for help but all to no avail. The faculty member had to try to pick another article. The publisher, many agreed, had missed a golden opportunity to revive the sales of a book.

NOTES

1. Grant Wiggins and Jay McTighe, *Understanding by Design* (Alexandria, VA: Association for Supervision and Curriculum Development, 1998).

2. For example, in the case of sound recordings, copyright owners may perform the work publicly by means of a digital audio transmission. See 17 U.S.C. §106 (2006).

3

TOOLS AND APPLICATIONS

Now that we have reviewed specific main features of massive open online courses (MOOCs), what are the basic technologies, tools, or applications that a library would use to build, edit, and deploy a MOOC? MOOCs, just like any other online learning course, can be created through a variety of technologies that vary by cost, complexity, and ease of use. In this chapter we will cover the various tools for creating different types of MOOCs, from the most basic, fiscally affordable MOOCs to super-MOOCs, using more expansive technologies. First, we need to define characteristics of these three categories of MOOCs, including technology and cost.

MODEST MOOCS, MODERATE MOOCS, AND SUPER MOOCS

Modest MOOCs ($0 to $500 investment)

MOOCs do not have to be million-dollar enterprises in order to be successful. Some of the most successful MOOCs result from an interesting topic combined with an engaging lecture and featuring clear audio and video content. A basic modest MOOC (mM) could be created for "free," utilizing staff, technology, free resources on the Internet, and expertise that is already located in the library. Arguably, some libraries could still benefit from some basic technology to make a modest

MOOC. Therefore, a library may have to make a small three-hundred-dollar investment to get the equipment it needs to create even the most modest of MOOCs.

Moderate MOOCs ($501 to $3,000)

For those organizations that have a solid budget line to explore MOOC-like initiatives, you can make a very polished, very engaging moderate MOOC (MM) with a budget going up to three thousand dollars. There is a lot of fiscal room in this moderate MOOC category. Cameras may be better, video software may offer more options, and you can afford to host the MOOC, potentially, on your own blog or website with a subscription to your own learning management system (LMS). The financial range in this category gives you lots of choices. And we will review several categories later.

Super MOOCs ($3,001 and up)

This last category of MOOCs is where the sky is nearly the limit. Many of the super MOOCs (SMs) are supported by funding from universities, government grants, and corporations, both for-profit and nonprofit. Academic libraries located within colleges and universities often provide good examples of super MOOCs. Again, we will explore, through examples, the equipment, software, and staffing that is used at this funding level.

Overview for Funding MOOCs: mM, MM, and SM

Regardless of what level of funding your library can provide, a key element for any MOOC is a thoughtful topic with an engaging lecture. Even if you spend fifteen thousand dollars on a MOOC, it may fail to engage with an audience. Again, price may not make much of a difference if you have a passionate lecturer, an engaging topic, and the ability for the participants to interact and learn along with the library.

Technical Equipment

Let's look at each category of technical equipment that may be necessary for a MOOC, briefly looking at the main features, uses, and estimated prices. Note that you can pick and choose different technologies in these categories and ultimately select what matches your library's MOOC budget—from mMs to MMs through SMs. This is by no means a complete tally of all the hardware and software available to make a MOOC. This list represents some of the technologies that have been used to create MOOCs at other institutions and can give you further ideas on the realities of creating a MOOC at your library.

Recording Video   One of the main features of a MOOC is the ability to share a presentation video. While you have a multitude of options to upload the videos (YouTube, Vimeo, Google Drive, etc.), you have to take the first step and actually capture the MOOC video first. The following are some video-capture options, with varying features for editing, postproduction, and audio.

Cameras   A camera is a big decision for a MOOC instructor. It can affect both content quality of the MOOC and considerations of the MOOC budget. The amount of choices available to consumers in the camera market is vast and daunting. A library that wants to offer a MOOC and purchase a new camera should ask, Will I rely on the library laptop/smartphone camera, or will we be purchasing a web, external, or professional grade studio camera? As you can imagine, these questions can lead to significant financial questions as well. Other questions involve features of many of these cameras: How high must the quality of video be? Do I need zoom lens capabilities, for close-ups and wide-shots? Do I need an additional external microphone, or is one built in to the camera? (And will that built-in mic be good enough for all types of video shoots?) Let's examine some of the options available, with a few concrete examples from the current market.

Built-in camera (mM, cost almost nothing). Today, the majority of laptops (and smartphones) are equipped with cameras. Theses cameras offer reliable quality and immediate integration into the video-recording software of your choice. Additionally, these built-in cameras often come with their own microphone, so there is no need for additional technology.

- Nearly all Windows laptops come with built-in cameras. For example, HP laptops come with the HP TrueVision HD Webcam with dual digital microphone. MacBook, MacBook Air, and MacBook Pro computers all feature an iSight HD camera (even iPhone 5s and some iPhone 4s incorporate an "iSight" rear camera as well as a front-facing Mac "FaceTime HD" camera). These cameras (and built-in microphones) can easily serve as the technology needed to record part or all of a MOOC, even for the most budget-conscious instructor. Often these cameras come with complimentary software for editing video captured.

External web camera (mM to MM, cost $99.99). Many MOOCs have opted for slightly better recording cameras attached to their computer. Even though many PCs and Macs come with built-in cameras, filming with an external webcam may give you more options for range, high definition, alternate perspectives, angles, and other positions. Depending on the style of video you are shooting (see chapter 5's section on "Video Production Format"), an external webcam may be your best option both for fiscal and format reasons.

- For example, a few MOOCs have used the "Logitech HD Pro Webcam C920, 1080 p Widescreen Video" with great success. This all-around web camera uses Carl Zeiss optics with full HD 1080 p recordings. Like most webcams, it features multiple mounting options, with a universal monitor clip and tripod-ready base. And much like the built-in web cameras, this eternal web camera comes with a built-in mic, so there's no need to purchase additional audio technology.

External digital camera (MM–SM, approximate cost $250–$4,000). For the same reasons you may want to use a web camera, you may also want to consider a higher-end digital camera. There is a range of manufactures, styles, components, and features that are available for digital cameras. Today, the majority offer a package that includes some sort of high-definition filming capability, their own batteries/power sources, lens options, and software. The price range on these models can be a few hundred to tens of thousands. However, a standard digital camera will do wonders, as long as it meets your quality standards and has power zoom action. Note that when purchasing a camera of this quality, a sturdy tripod is essential. This may add to the cost, but any tripod that is designed to hold two times the weight of your camera setup should be fine.

- For example, a camera in the affordable range, used by a few MOOCs, is the Flip UltraHD Video Camera. This camera is part of a style of "shoot-and-share" digital cameras with image stabilization and superior HD. It has a basic interface, and there is no need to be a professional photographer to take advantage of the many features the Flip camera offers. Depending on the memory size of the camera, you can record between two and six hours of HD video. And when you're done recording, you can simply connect the Flip camera via its USB arm to a PC or Mac and use the preloaded FlipShare software to organize and edit the MOOC videos. The software automatically organizes each video in a simple drop-and-drag folder interface. The editing software is simple to use and, again, free with the camera. Like other external cameras, it comes with a rechargeable power source.
- Another example, more toward the SM end of the pricing spectrum, is a camera for a professional, "in-studio" shoot. For example, MOOCs being filmed in-studio at HarvardX use a Canon EOS C100 camera. This is a high-end, multifunctional camera optimized for use by videographers, documentarians, and independent filmmakers. It films in high resolution 1080 p, with enhanced autofocusing, a superior built-in microphone, and a host of other features. You can, of course, use it in the most basic settings, since the camera provides a continuous, nonstop recording function and the ability to create "in and out points" in the footage every time the start/stop button is pressed, and it will still create a professional-quality MOOC video. Obviously, this camera is pricey.

Screencasting   Screencasting is a great option for MOOC classes. Libraries, specifically, can utilize screencasts as a MOOC production tool for the "show and tell" portion of their learning modules. The participant can see exactly what is happening on the instructor's screen, step by step, as made famous in the Khan Academy style of MOOC videos. Fortunately, the market has a great deal of affordable software available to capture MOOC screencasts. Let's examine some of the options available, with a few concrete examples from the current market.

- Open Broadcaster Software (OBS) (mM, free download for Windows). OBS has been called the best free screencasting and streaming tool available on the web. Initially it was developed in the gaming community as a video-streaming tool so others could view a screencast in real time. However, OBS added a "local stream" option, which creates a video file, so that you can save and upload the videos for your MOOC. It is an open-source program, so you can go behind the scenes and make real technical adjustments if you'd like. The interface is not as simple as some of the drag-and-drop programs reviewed below, but it has many powerful features for a free program. You can add image and text overlays to your video output. It gives you options for multiple sources for picture-in-picture, audio recording, and other choices. Again, because it is an open-source program, the learning curve can be steep for screencasting novices. However, OBS added something called a "settings estimator" that will approximate the right settings based on your computer specifications. This will both ease the learning curve and get OBS up and running more quickly, so you can get to screencasting video creation faster.
- Screencast-O-Matic (mM, free download Windows or Mac, Pro version $15). Many reviewers think Screencast-O-Matic is the perfect balance of features, ease of use, and price (free). There is both a Mac and Windows version, but the Windows version lets you launch the program with a Java applet without installing any software on your computer. It records your webcam as well as your screen at the same time and lets you select the size of that recording window in a drag-and-drop interface. Videos can be saved to your computer as an MP4 and uploaded directly to YouTube. While free, it will limit you to fifteen minutes and puts a small "Screencast-O-Matic" watermark in the lower left corner of the final published video. However, the Pro version, which has a number of features and is watermark free, costs a mere fifteen dollars a year. It is truly an excellent bargain for a screencasting program with so many features. The Pro version also gives you

video-editing options and the ability to record for longer than fifteen minutes. It also records videos in higher definition, allows publishing in more video formats, and has a great deal of new features released monthly. For the price, even at the fifteen-dollar Pro level, this is well worth a download.

- iMovie (mM, free with Mac). iMovie is a basic video-editing software application made by Apple for Macs, iPads, and iPhones. It is included free with all new Mac computers, so if your library has a Mac, then you already have what you need to get started with this program. iMovie has a simple drag-and-drop interface, so as you are recording various clips on your Mac, you can cobble them together in the iMovie time line and arrange them however you like. You have the ability to make picture-in-picture and side-by-side effects and apply audio overlays (including your own narration or iMovie's unique access to Apple's built-in sound effects library, iTunes, or GarageBand). They have even recently added an update for green-screen effects to superimpose the MOOC instructor over photo and video backgrounds. Recently, iMovie has upgraded a specific feature, which will help with marketing your MOOC: movie trailer software. Based on your MOOC videos and photos, you choose a specific ready-made trailer template, and the software adds graphics and original scores automatically. You can customize your library logos, cast names, and credits. The system helps you select the best videos and photos for your MOOC trailer with the help of their featured "drop zones." So iMovie, with all its basic features, makes a good option for quality MOOCs at a fiscally responsible price.
- Jing (mM, free download for Windows or Mac). Jing is a free and easy-to-use screencasting program from TechSmith, which also makes the more advanced Camtasia (review below). It has a simple drag-and-record interface that allows you to record small or large portions of your screen for simple screenshots or screencast videos. Jing also provides free online storage from its partner program Screencast.com, which gives users 2 GB of server space for free. After recording, you can add text, notes, and arrows, or highlight important sections. With the free version, you can only share the link to the stored screencast, which pulls up a new window with a Flash video on it. This video can be watched on this screen,

but you can't embed the video itself anywhere else. If you want the ability to upload and download the videos to your own drive, YouTube, Vimeo, and so forth, then TechSmith suggests you upgrade from free Jing to SnagIt. SnagIt is very similar to Jing, with an easy-to-use interface, but provides you with additional features, such as the ability to record longer videos (over five minutes), blur sensitive information, scroll up and down on screencast web pages, and much more. You can use SnagIt for free for fifteen days, and the full version (which you pay for only once) is $49.95. Lastly, TechSmith does have excellent written and video tutorials available to help users with questions about either Jing or SnagIt.

- ScreenFlow5 (mM to MM, cost $99.99). ScreenFlow5 is both video-recording software and a video editor. ScreenFlow5 will let you screencast a MOOC; zoom in and out on the screen; and add callouts, titles, annotations, transitions, and video and audio actions, all in one software package. While not as fancy as large, more expensive programs, such as Final Cut Pro or Adobe Premiere, you can capture and edit MOOC video very easily once you get the hang of the system. ScreenFlow5, truly, is at its best when it is screencasting. For example, when you attach an iPhone or iPad to your Mac, that device becomes a capture source, right along with your Mac's screen and any compatible cameras. As it captures the device's video, ScreenFlow automatically grabs any audio it plays as well. The software lets you combine multiple input sources. For example, you could choose to capture a Mac's display, an iPad, narration from a connected microphone, and video from your Mac's iSight HD camera. Most sources are added as separate tracks. There is a slight learning curve for the editing part of the software. It has many unique features and functions, and is quite good for MOOC work. For example, ScreenFlow5 lets you insert markers both during recording and as you edit, so that you may later go back to cut your clip at this point or add an action.
- Camtasia 8 (mM to MM, cost $299.99 Windows, $99.99 Mac). Camtasia is powerful video-capture and editing software. It is such a good system that it is equally as popular with professional video-production workers as with those who are creating MOOCs.

This is probably due to the fact that Camtasia also gives you the ability to add quizzes and other interactive elements more common to a MOOC, and the process has been simplified in the latest edition, Camtasia 8. You can now offer multiple choice, fill in the blank, true/false, and short answer questions. Camtasia also offers several recording tools and a full complement of editing tools, as well as a large number of file-conversion formats. You can capture any activity on your computer screen and create videos, presentations, demonstrations and tutorials, personal screencasts, and other projects. Record from a webcam; record a screencast; record from a collection of images, animations, or audio and video elements that you place on the time line; or mix any of the above for a true multimedia MOOC. You can import camera video, music, photos, and other media. With Camtasia Studio, you can cut, splice, and combine clips easily. For those with ready-to-go PowerPoint slide decks, Camtasia offers a special PowerPoint add-in, so that you can take advantage of the work you may have already done for a non-MOOC class. For the $299 price for Windows-based computers you get a host of these incredible editing and recording features. If the price seems too expensive, why not try Camtasia's thirty-day trial? Not only will your library get to use the best version of Camtasia, but also you get to try out and learn the program's features for free. Note that the less expensive Camtasia Mac product has fewer features and therefore is set at the lower price. The Windows version is far superior and worth at least the thirty-day trial.

Software
- Windows Movie Maker (mM, free for Windows computers). Windows Movie Maker is part of the free Windows Essential Download (including Mail, OneDrive, and more). This free video-editing software's true advantage is its simplicity. You can easily combine video clips into larger movies with features such as titles, transitions, background music, and effects. Movie Maker uses a video editor time line system, with clips represented by thumbnails, which you can easily combine, cut, and trim. Want to import a voiceover? Movie Maker lets you use any MP3, WAV, M4A, or WMA files to import into the video. You can even add background music that is recommended for

certain "themes" you can apply to videos—default, contemporary, cinematic, fade, pan and zoom (best used with photos), black and white, and sepia.

- Adobe Premiere Pro (APP, MM to SM, cost Cloud version: $29.99/ month; cost for one computer: $299.99/year). The first step when creating any video project with Premiere Pro is capturing or importing your video footage, audio, and other elements into the software. Importing media that's already on your computer is the most straightforward, and capturing files from digital media, such as from your camera or other devices, is similarly simple. There is even a MOOC on Udemy on learning this system called "Learn Adobe Premiere Pro: Video Editing Like a Professional" (https://www.udemy. com/adobe-premiere-pro/). Note that APP is now part of Adobe Creative Cloud subscription service. Now instead of paying one lump sum for a specific Adobe suite of tools, you now have to pay monthly (or annually in some cases). The upside is you won't have to purchase a specific release ever again, as upgrades are included.

- Final Cut Pro X (MM to SM, cost $299.99). Final Cut Pro X (FCPX) looks a bit like its cheaper counterpart program, iMovie, with its basic "time line" view, but that is where the comparison ends. Professionals and MOOC creators alike agree that FCPX is one of the most powerful video-editing tools on the market; it handles editing, audio, and effects better than any other software and is well worth the price. Final Cut offers precise, intuitive, and powerful tools for arranging and trimming clips. Trimming and splitting can be done in the "time line" or right in the clip's iMovie-like source. It has a simple drag-and-drop interface for editing, and once your clips are all in place, you can enhance them with color tools, transitions, effects, and text tools. Crop, rotate, resize, and move video simply and easily. FCPX's chroma-keying program is second to none and allows you to take full advantage of any green-screen effects, from basic color backdrops to high-resolution "location shoots"—all in the comfort of your own library. The new audio features automatically fix hum, noise, and noise spikes (also a manual adjustment, if necessary), and they have over one thousand open-source sound effects to utilize. With some practice, and a little experimentation, a library can get up to speed on the many interesting and multifaceted features of FCPX. For the price, it may be worth the library investment.

Recording Audio   A camera will generally have a built-in microphone. The range, clarity, and quality of that captured audio might be fine for home videos but not for the library's MOOC. No matter where a MOOC has been produced, the audio will always be listed as the first- or second-most important element (the other is video). Why? Because you can't learn from a MOOC without hearing the instructor. Although a MOOC may have excellent visuals, the audio is critical to all aspects of a MOOC, from screencasting to in-classroom lectures. If you have the budget, it is highly recommended that you get a microphone of some sort. Again, this is an area where you can spend easily into the thousands, but here, we will review some moderate options that will capture some quality audio.

- Blue Snowball USB Microphone (mM to MM, cost $59.99). This seems to be the "go-to" affordable mic in the world of music, podcasts, and MOOCs. It is a must-have for reasonably budgeted MOOC screencasts. It's a direct plug-and-play mic that connects to either a Mac or PC and does not need any additional software. Plus, the microphone is bus powered from USB, so no batteries are required. It stands on a mini tripod right at your desk, podium, or office. On the back there is a three-position switch that lets you adjust how the audio is captured: (1) directional for speech, vocals, and podcasting; (2) cardioid capsule for live music and loud sound sources; and (3) omnidirectional for conferences and interviews. It is about the size of a grapefruit, so you need a little room to set it up. But other than that, for the price, the sound quality is excellent.
- Blue Yeti USB Microphone (MM-SM, cost $129.99). Another excellent plug-and-play microphone for the price, this Yeti microphone has more features and makes better studio-quality recordings than its less expensive cousin, the Blue Snowball. It features four different pattern settings for recoding record vocals, podcasts, or interviews in ways that would normally require multiple microphones. It includes more buttons and features on the mic itself, so that you can adjust settings on the go. For example, if you are experiencing distortion or feedback while recording an especially loud source, you can adjust the gain control on the mic. Or tap the instant mute button, when you are worried about outside

sound. The microphone comes equipped with a headphone jack that allows you to listen to what you're recording in real time. If you have the budget, this microphone will be a huge addition to your MOOC equipment arsenal.

- Zoom H4n Audio Recorder (MM to SM, cost $199.99). The H4n has been used by professional videographers for years and is a high-quality four-track recorder for the price. If you are recording a MOOC video with a DSLR or other professional high-grade camera, the H4n is the perfect complement. It can be connected to any standard tripod or mic stand, or you can use Zoom's adapter to mount it directly to your DSLR camera, capturing with clarity the MOOC video you are shooting. The interface is digital and includes an X/Y recording feature that would benefit MOOC videos capturing a classroom, a panel, or an interview while still capturing sound sources in the center of the shoot with clarity and definition. It comes with a 1 GB SD card, windscreen, mic clip adapter, AC adapter, USB cable, protective case, and its own optional recording software. Battery life is six to eleven hours per charge.

Lighting   Lighting is one of the major components of a video shoot that truly affects the overall quality of the MOOC. With some simple lighting, you can avoid the dark, hazy look of a homegrown YouTube video and instead mimic the look of a polished, well-lit studio production. Lighting can make the basic web cameras look as good as a studio shoot—it is often just ignored on many videos we see on the Internet today.

For example, if you are using the "floating head" method of MOOC videos, isn't it critical that you light the face of the instructor? If you are doing a shoot in the library stacks, isn't it critical that you set the backlight to illuminate the stacks clearly? These considerations about lighting should be made when you are first planning your MOOC shoots and can ease the nuisance of fixing the lighting later in the video-editing software.

A lot of the complexities of lighting can be solved through using basic lamps that would be available in any library, office, or home. As you know, the range of quality of lamps depends a lot on the manufacturer, the light bulbs used, and the wattage. Experiment with what works best. Many of the web cameras, video cameras, and video-editing software includes the ability to adjust for lighting, so you can see immediately during a test shoot if you need more or less light. Another simple solution may be a ready-to-go studio light kit.

- Video Studio Kit 1600 watt—Complete Video Solution (MM to SM, cost $199.00). This lighting kit, sold by TubeTape (http://www.tubetape.net/), has been used by a number of MOOCs to get the correct lighting at a fraction of the cost of a full studio production light set. The "Complete Video Solution" kit includes two professional-grade lights, adjustable light stands, basic light bulbs, and a carrying case for the equipment. This kit even includes a green-screen backdrop with stand, for MOOCs that want to experiment with green-screen technologies available in some of the video-editing software. In fact, the kit even includes its own video software package, in case you find their software meets your MOOC needs better.

Other   There are a few technologies that lie outside the above categories but nevertheless would make a fine addition to a MOOC production.

- Green Screens (MM to SM, free with TubeTape lighting kit, or approximately $25.99). Green screens are used as part of a technique called chroma keying. This technique allows you to take a portion of the background (or the entire background) and replace it with a new image. After using a green screen to create a filmed background of a single solid color—often a nice hue of green or blue—you can tell the editing software to replace everything that is green or blue with a different image. This can be done in post-production or even in real time (like the television weathermen with their maps and moving charts). The software programs such as Adobe Premiere and Final Cut Pro X have built-in features that work with video green-screen effects. If you are feeling comfortable with the technology, you can even use whole images in the background, such as scenes from a library (if you can't shoot in the stacks) or exotic locations (film yourself in Italy by using a background from Rome).

- Flex iPad Teleprompter (SM, cost $899.99 and up). For those MOOC productions that are on the level of television studio productions, a teleprompter is a nice tool to work with. If you have a teleprompter, you are less likely to skip the "scripting" position of the MOOC planning process. The Flex iPad Teleprompter works with an iPad to easily and readily display words to the instructor in a fully controlled and customized pace. The font, color, texture, and background of the teleprompter are all customizable to what works for the instructor's vision. It does take a little getting used to—talking and reading with a level of enthusiasm—but with some practice, it can sound very professional. Speech patterns change when you use a teleprompter, and instructors will definitely exhibit fewer awkward pauses, "ums," or other hitches that delay recording time.

LEARNING MANAGEMENT SYSTEMS

If you are considering a MOOC for your library, another early determination should be which tool you will use to build the course itself. Fortunately, over the last three years, a number of good options have developed for MOOC instructors looking to build their own MOOCs. The following is an assessment of selected, popular, free MOOC (and MOOC-like) platforms, or as we will call them, learning management systems (LMSs). These selected reviews were created with the aid of John Swope. John is the founder of Curricu.me (http://solutions. curricu.me/), a full-service consultancy that helps organizations build enterprise-quality online courses.[1]

Udemy LMS

Udemy is one of the simpler online education platforms that allows individual instructors to build courses that they can either charge for or offer for free. (Some classes have over ten thousand paying students.) Udemy hosts the courses in the cloud, and building on the platform requires no coding knowledge. It can be thought of as a presentation platform like Slideshare but enhanced with voice-over, quizzes, and forum capabilities. Courses are very easy to set up. Most teachers up-

Figure 3.1. *Courtesy of John Swope and curricu.me*

load a PowerPoint and record a voice-over, with multiple-choice questions at the end of each unit. You can also upload video, audio recording, and documents.

A Udemy course must be accessed via the Udemy.com site, so branding options are limited. A MOOC cannot be white labeled or use a custom domain. But Udemy does have two million registered users on their site, and they often do things to promote popular new courses.

Strengths

- Ease of setup
- Udemy's audience of two million users

Weaknesses

- Free version is not brandable
- Limited student analytics

Most appropriate for

- Individual instructors who want to monetize their courses

CourseSites by Blackboard

CourseSites is a more full-featured online course platform that is also cloud based and requires no coding knowledge. CourseSites is more specifically geared toward instructors within educational institutions. In addition to basic MOOC functionality, it offers features like Course Announcements, Awards/Badges, and a "Grading Center."

The advantage to CourseSites may be the familiarity with the Blackboard system, which is a standard LMS used at many schools around the world. The familiarity with Blackboard can make for an easy transition from classroom to MOOC for many librarians, faculty, and staff. One state university, Colorado State University, already very familiar with Blackboard, is now converting their existing distance-education infrastructure into open courses using CourseSites.[2]

CourseSites feels, in every way, like a tool for use in the classroom. From the student's perspective, a dashboard shows announcements, to-dos, and a calendar. These features seem ideal for a student trying to keep track of multiple assignments across several classes. But it feels overwhelming for a nonclassroom audience that is likely only taking one MOOC and less interested in grading or deadlines. Nonetheless, Cour-

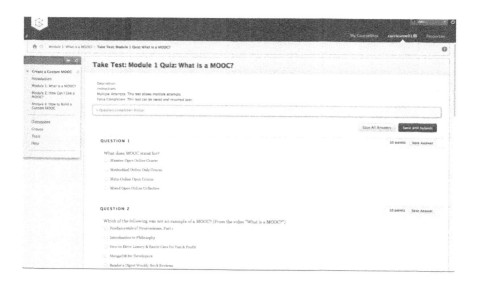

Figure 3.2.   *Courtesy of John Swope and curricu.me*

seSites provides one of the best combinations of full functionality and ease of setup.

Strengths

- Full featured
- Easy setup

Weaknesses

- Not brandable
- Limit of five courses

Most appropriate for

- Individual teachers who want to build classes online

Versal

Versal is an intriguing new platform. Its major strengths are a sleek, intuitive user interface and a robust drag-and-drop functionality. A user can sign up for free and then build a course that includes mathematical expressions, image drill-downs, and many more widgets, all without any coding knowledge. Users can also embed their published courses on other websites, such as personal blogs.

Versal can't fairly be called a MOOC platform, because it lacks certain MOOC elements. In particular, there is currently no forum or discussion functionality. Instead, it can be thought of as a strong tutorial platform.

Versal is most suited to individuals who want to quickly build sleek tutorials—for example, teachers who build assignments for their students or musicians who build short courses on music theory and post it on their blogs. Versal is a young product, and the company is planning to develop some of the features that its platform currently lacks. This is one to keep an eye on.

Strengths

- Ease of use

Figure 3.3. *Courtesy of John Swope and curricu.me*

- Advanced drag-and-drop widgets (e.g., 3-D modeling and virtual piano exercises)

Weaknesses

- No forum capabilities

Most appropriate for

- Individual instructors who want to deliver tutorials to existing audiences

Moodle

Moodle has been around for over ten years and is one of the most popular open-source course management solutions available. As such, it is not specifically a MOOC platform but a competent online course platform that can handle large classrooms, and a lot of the open online

Figure 3.4.   *Courtesy of John Swope and curricu.me*

classes you may have seen that are not affiliated with the major plat-forms were built on Moodle.

The great strength of Moodle is its combination of full functionality with extensive customization options. Moodle offers all the basic course elements plus fairly advanced elements like SCORM compliance and group permissions. Because Moodle is open source, users have the ability to customize nearly everything within their implementation if they know where to look.

Moodle requires a self-hosted installation, but building simple courses is fairly intuitive and requires no coding knowledge. The trade-off is that the platform is over ten years old. Because of its robustness, the advanced options can be daunting at times. Luckily, the Moodle community is extremely active, and most questions can be solved via a quick search in the instructor forums.

Strengths

- Open source
- Highly expandable and customizable

Weaknesses

- Performance intensive
- Requires setup and maintenance investment

Most appropriate for

- Schools or small/medium organizations that want a full-featured learning management system

Open edX

You may know edX as the platform where MOOCs faculty from very selective universities are hosted. But the software behind it, developed by Harvard and MIT, was released as open source in March 2013, enabling anyone to use the full-featured platform, which is dedicated specifically to building MOOCs. EdX's apparent goal is to become the WordPress of online course platforms, where users can start with a basic framework and then add functionality via third-party plug-ins.

Figure 3.5. *Courtesy of John Swope and curricu.me*

The edX course-building platform is the same tool used by the universities who offer MOOCs on edX.org. If you've taken an edX.org MOOC, you have a basic idea of what this platform can offer. Students can watch lectures, take multiple kinds of quizzes, participate in forums, and even work on labs or cooperative essays. Creating basic courses can all be done via edX Studio—a graphical user interface for course creators—and multiple instructors can work on a course together.

EdX does require a self-hosted installation, though they have recently developed a fairly easy-to-use AWS install. In return for the time it takes to set up and maintain your edX instance, you get full access to your student data and unlimited customization options.

Strengths

- Open source
- Fully brandable and customizable
- Designed to handle large classrooms (one hundred thousand plus)

Weaknesses

- Requires setup and maintenance investment

Most appropriate for

- Organizations that want a sleek, modern online course tool, potentially for very large student audiences

Open Online Education with Course Builder by Google

Made by one of the biggest Internet companies in the world, this platform contains software and instructions for presenting your materials in a MOOC. You can organize the material into lessons, activities, and tests. It is fully integrated with the other Google suite of applications (Drive, Groups, Gmail, etc.) to create an instant MOOC community.

However, it is not a simple setup. Instructors may need to have a good understanding of HTML and JavaScript to deploy their MOOC with Course Builder. Also, Google Course Builder requires participants (and instructors) to have a Google account to register for any MOOC setup on the platform.

Lastly, while Google has committed to maintaining this platform, as of 2014 they will be "focusing development efforts on Open edX" as part of a development deal between Google and edX. In other words, if you chose Google Course Builder, don't expect any upgrades or new features.

Strengths

- Ease and simplicity of integration with Google's other suite of applications—you can integrate your MOOC with Google Drive, Google Groups, and so forth.

Weaknesses

- Google Course Builder page is not exactly user-friendly; some complex directions for MOOC setup
- If you choose Course Builder, don't expect any upgrades or new features, since Google has stopped development to work more closely with edX on a new MOOC platform.

Most appropriate for

- Advanced MOOC instructors with some coding or development background

Desire2Learn's Open Courses

Canada's Desire2Learn (D2L) recently launched Open Courses, which provides a full suite of LMS tools and allows each institution to define a MOOC, control the course direction, award "certified credit" for participation, and import content quickly and easily. D2L Open Courses platform is also available as a standalone cloud implementation. D2L offers an integrated solution with a host of features that integrate some of the most common applications used by MOOC participants. For example, D2L Open Courses integrates with the most popular collaboration tools, like Google Docs. It can also integrate modules from Microsoft's Office 365 and many, many Google Apps.

D2L Open Courses also developed "Binder," a mobile and web-based app that lets MOOC participants access and work with content from courses, digital textbooks, and online storage services such as Dropbox or SkyDrive. The University System of Georgia is among the institutions that have tested the MOOC platform and have been pleased with the outcome. Open Courses hopes to introduce more interactive elements that they theorize will keep MOOC enrollment rates high and lower the dropout rate.

Strengths

- Ease and simplicity of integration of Open Courses is built on the same D2L technology that instructors are already using
- Full integration with common participant apps such as Office 365 and Google Apps

Weaknesses

- Requires setup and maintenance investment with D2L; can't just launch your own MOOC immediately

Most appropriate for

- Organizations that want to fully invest into a new and technically integrated MOOC for large student audiences

LearnDash

LearnDash is quickly becoming a secret weapon for individuals and institutions that want to launch a MOOC using software that they can trust. It is a supplemental WordPress MOOC platform add-on that was designed by individuals with backgrounds in the e-learning space, and therefore is very adaptable to a wide variety of MOOC pedagogical needs. Like WordPress, it is easy to install, learn, and implement. The real benefit is that many libraries have used and are familiar with the WordPress layout, so the learning curve will be low for MOOC instructors.

To start, it works with any WordPress theme so you can customize the look and feel of your MOOC. The software is designed so that

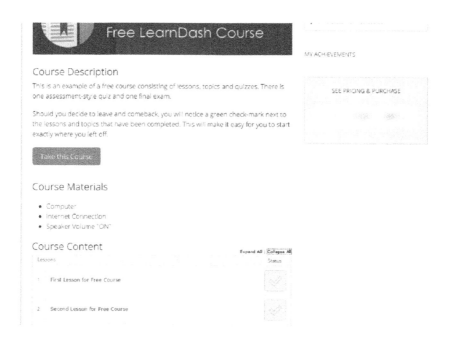

Figure 3.6.

instructors can easily create an unlimited number of courses, lessons, and topics. The class functions manage all of the people who have registered for your MOOC. The platform for uploading videos or other MOOC files is simple, and only registered users can view your content.

Strengths

- Ease and simplicity of integration with WordPress, for a very reasonable price
- All the MOOC content can be made and organized on the site: courses, lessons, topics, videos, quizzes, and certificates.

Weaknesses

- You will have to learn the lingo and workflow for creating a class, but it is not a huge learning curve.

Most appropriate for

- Individuals, libraries, or small/medium organizations that want a full-featured LMS for their MOOC

Conclusion

Which platform you choose depends on what assumptions you make about your course. Most of these platforms offer demos on their site. It helps to be able to play around in a course and try to imagine your content with a similar look and feel. Finally, don't worry about changing your mind early on. These platforms all rely on much of the same content (YouTube videos, PDFs, quizzes, etc.), so it is easy to migrate a course halfway through the building process. With some effort and patience, you can put out a MOOC that is on par with some of the university MOOCs that are available.

NOTES

1. John Swope is the founder of Curricu.me (http://solutions.curricu.me/), an online MOOC aggregator that allows users to build and share custom curriculum with their students, employees, and friends. His favorite MOOC is Dan Ariely's "Beginner's Guide to Irrational Behavior," and his personal blog (http://www.johnswope.com/) takes much inspiration from Ariely's theories around irrational economics. You can follow him on Twitter as well at https://twitter.com/j_swope00.

2. Read more about Colorado's experiences with CourseSites and MOOCs in Robert McGuire, "Using 'Traditional' Online Education to Launch MOOCs: A Q&A with Colorado State's Distance Ed Team," MOOC News and Reviews, September 5, 2013, accessed December 5, 2014, http://moocnewsandreviews.com/.

4

LIBRARY EXAMPLES AND CASE STUDIES

In this chapter we are going to examine exactly how libraries and librarians are getting involved in massive open online courses (MOOCs). From behind-the-scenes work to out in front of the camera, many librarians have found interesting and dynamic roles to aid the MOOC phenomena at their institutions.

EXAMPLES OF THE DIFFERENT WAYS LIBRARIES ARE SUPPORTING MOOCS

Copyright Risk Assessment

When MOOCs first started involving libraries in planning, one major role that emerged was in the copyright arena. As previously discussed, the use of copyrighted third-party materials may be critical to the MOOC pedagogy, especially in humanities classes. How can you teach a music MOOC without some music? How can you teach a Van Gogh MOOC without some of his paintings? Libraries have been on the forefront of helping MOOC instructors ensure the materials they use to create their MOOC presentations are not going to subject them to the risk of copyright infringement. As patrons have done in the past, MOOC instructors are increasingly turning to the library for help with copyright. The earlier the library is involved in this process, the better.

The whole concept boils down to this simple fact: the fair-use exemption does not always apply to the MOOC environment as it does for in-classroom teaching. Although instructors may or may not be aware of that fact, they certainly are made aware when it comes time to collect the content for their MOOCs. Add into the equation the profit and nonprofit status of some MOOC enterprises (edX is a nonprofit, mostly at educational institutions, Coursera and Udacity are for-profit companies) and fair-use rights are pushed a bit further back. Lastly, these MOOCs are distributing (a right of the copyright owner) at a scale unprecedented for the classroom environment, so the risk of massive copyright infringement is even higher.

Librarians are in the best position to have copyright expertise on the use of materials in these MOOCs and, additionally, may be in the best position to research the rights status of the works, or suggest alternate materials that would serve the same purpose. Librarians are often in charge of, or intimately involved with, open-access repositories or other freely licensed materials in their subject area. Librarians are aware of the advantages of linking to resources, through the creation of research guides, research pathfinders, and e-reserves work.

There is also an open-access advocacy role that arises naturally from these library copyright consultations. The limiting nature of MOOCs and using copyrighted materials helps drive many of the open educational resources and open-access discussions. Instructors are realizing that the publishing contracts they have signed for an article may be effecting their scholarly distribution channels, and MOOCs often exemplify that conflict. Instructors will see the need to make their own writings accessible to their MOOC participants worldwide and may influence their MOOC colleagues to do the same. We will discuss a bit more about open-access possibilities in a later chapter.

Either way, copyright and licensing librarians are doing what they do best, providing information to their patrons to make decisions and, through the lens of the law, mitigating the risk on the library or institution launching the MOOC.

Teaching

Librarians are also getting out in front of the camera in many MOOCs. Many different programs rely heavily on library support for teaching on-ground classes. When a class is moved online, sometimes that support has to move online as well. With the advent of MOOCs, librarians are finding themselves stepping into familiar teaching roles and, occasionally, unfamiliar roles.

So far, these roles tend to come in three varieties: information and subject expertise, instruction, and behind-the-scenes work.

Information and Subject Expertise

Typically it is subject specialist librarians who have the greatest knowledge of their own collections—who better to share information about those collections? When a MOOC is collection or subject focused, we have seen a variety of examples where librarians are called upon to film a segment to share their collection expertise.

For example, edX launched a class titled "MCB80x Fundamentals of Neuroscience," taught by Professor David Cox, assistant professor of molecular and cellular biology and of computer science. In his class, Cox wanted to work with the preserved skull of Phineas Gage, a railroad worker who, in 1848, had a thirteen-pound tamping iron rod blown straight through his skull (and frontal lobe) in an accident. Phineas lived, and the case is famous as the first medical knowledge gained on the relationship between personality and the functioning of the brain's frontal lobe.

The skull and tamping iron were donated to the Warren Anatomical Museum at Harvard University. Dominic Hall is currently the curator of that collection, which resides inside at Harvard's Countway Library of Medicine. With an expert already on hand, Cox decided to let Dominic lecture about the skull and Phineas Gage, as well as share knowledge about Phineas's life, his famous accident, and how the library eventually came to own this unique piece of neuroscience history.

Dominic's lecture takes up the majority of the segment, with questions from Cox to drive the discussion. In this way, the library becomes part of the class and accomplishes at least one goal that every MOOC should have: share the unique collections and expertise of both the library and the librarian. Not only did Dominic get to share information about the collection, but he has also contributed to further understanding of Phineas's role in the examination of the human brain. This concept would be revisited throughout the class.

Figure 4.1.   Dominic Hall, lecturing in NeuroscienceX *Source:* **HarvardX.**

In-Library MOOC Delivery and Support

The library institution itself, including staff, technology, and facilities, is well positioned to deliver any support that would aid participants to engage with online courses. This support does not need to come from an edX or Coursera institution; rather, it can come from a public library in a participant's city or town.

For example, in August 2014, the New York Public Library (NYPL) offered its first program on creating a "blended library learning environment," combining MOOC technology with in-person library support. The program was titled the "Learning Hubs Initiative." Participants (NYPL card holders) who signed up for the six-week MOOC "The Camera Never Lies" met each week for ninety minutes in the Grand Central or Mulberry Street NYPL branches in Manhattan, to discuss the class among peers, and with a library facilitator. The NYPL provided space called a "learning hub" for the participants.

The ultimate goal of the pilot was to try to combat the very high dropout rate for MOOCs, by providing an opportunity to develop a community around the class and an NYPL library facilitator to answer questions. The theory is that the Coursera/NYPL program gives participants "the edge" by including subject experts and a true classroom-like experience to keep the participants engaged and interested in completing the course. How did they keep the community alive? Each week, the NYPL tracked attendance and the engagement with the MOOCs materials. The first collaboration went so well that NYPL is offering another MOOC Learning Hubs Initiative with a Coursera poetry class and plans on more in-person support in the future.

Behind-the-Scenes Work

A great deal of work goes into getting a collection ready to be scanned, digitized, or filmed for use in a MOOC. Many libraries have been providing this kind of support for on-ground classes for years. With a MOOC, we are capable of sharing the most rare and wonderful treasures of our collections with the world, but occasionally, they need some work. This could be preservation work, binding work, digital enhancement, or a number of other processes. Often a MOOC will challenge the traditional "show-and-tell" model and use material in new and different ways. What if a MOOC was to capture all that behind-the-scenes work?

In preparation for the upcoming edX class, "HUM 1x: History of the Book," the Weissman Preservation Center, which provides long-term usability of Harvard's rare and unique collections, was called upon to coordinate preservation actions in preparation for digitization of certain works for use in the MOOC. They were working with some of Harvard Library's most rare and treasured materials.

HarvardX proposed that they not only include the Weissman experts in the video about these rare books but also promote the expert work that was being done at the center in support of the MOOC. The shoot took around two days and focuses on the analysis and treatment of medieval manuscripts (book and scroll) for the class. They interviewed professionals at the Weissman Preservation Center and revealed some of the techniques that were used in prepping the books for scanning. The video is short but powerful. We see that the center is made up of many professional staff members using brushes, microscopes, gold-leaf foil, and a variety of other tools and equipment.

Figure 4.2.   Weissman Preservation Center's video for HarvardX's "History of the Book" MOOC *Source:* HarvardX.

After the work was completed, and will be included in the upcoming class, there was a new side benefit that almost went unnoticed: campaign advertising and promotion for what Harvard Library does at the Weissman Preservation Center. Reusable videos such as these can serve a dual purpose: they are revealing and educational to the participants in the MOOC, and they serve as promotional marketing material for the library itself. Libraries, regardless of their size, often suffer from a lack of marketing and promotion. If we can harness the power and reputation of the MOOC, we can use these features, films, videos, and displays of our work to our benefit. As it stands now, the video filmed in the Weissman Preservation Center will be used in the University Capital Campaign for the Harvard Library.

Professional Development

In addition, libraries are exploring ways to use MOOCs for professional development and continuing education. Last fall, San Jose State University professor Michael Stephens taught one of the first library-themed MOOCs, "The Hyperlinked Library," and is exploring the use of MOOCs in the library courses at the university's library program.

There has always been a market for private, online learning and professional development, but the potential for MOOC-enabled, self-directed professional development is just starting to enter the world of libraries and librarianship. Later in the book, we have a chapter on setting up a sample internal MOOC for staff training.

MOOC Production Support

The twenty-first-century librarian has a lot of experience with teaching and technology. As the American Library Association notes each year, traditional job titles for librarians are shifting to reflect the more technical aspects of the job. Some of this technical know-how includes webinars, video production, and online learning expertise. In all of these cases, libraries are typically in a good position to support MOOC production. At academic institutions, faculty members use university equipment to create their MOOC. Software and computer programs may fall outside their expertise. Training these MOOC instructors, regardless of the institution, can fall within the teaching, learning, and research departments at any library. Many early adopting libraries have been experimenting with a MOOC-like flipped classroom environment. In fact, the instructional, skills-based nature of bibliographic instruction favors a flipped classroom. Why can't we simply move these library experts to also support the MOOC mission and its production? This is not to suggest that the library become the de-facto MOOC IT department for the institution (setting up and fixing technology—although many, many librarians do just that); rather, libraries can provide a different kind of instructional support—creating, editing, and deploying MOOCs using technology the library already has, or can acquire. Again, in this role it is critical that the library be "at the table" in the very beginning of a MOOC discussion.

Supporting MOOC Participants

The "elephant in the room" with any MOOC library discussion is the questions of supporting the MOOC participants, which can range from a small private online course (SPOC) of a few hundred to tens of thousands of participants. In the academic environment, one of the library's classic roles most analogous to MOOC participants is supporting the students that are in classes at their colleges and universities. Librarians also procure, make accessible, relay, teach, and archive resources related to these academic classes. At academic libraries, this support and production is usually limited to the students, faculty, and staff enrolled or employed at that institution.

The first question should be, do MOOC participants even need our support? MOOCs are typically shorter, skills-based or job-related classes that last from four to eight weeks. In classes such as these, traditionally, librarian involvement may be unnecessary. It is rare for a MOOC to assign a midterm paper or ask for individual research assignments (although some library MOOCs do have small research assignments, which we will review later). Ultimately, it is unclear whether these participants need library help.

Second, even if the participants do need library help, does an academic library use its time and money to support potential reference questions, or other questions, for the "nonpaying customer?" The bottom-line answer can simply be a combination of human and financial capital: if we allow tens of thousands of MOOC participants to do individual research and open the reference desk to question, the librarians would be overwhelmed and couldn't support either the on-campus or the MOOC patrons. It may not be worth the risk.

Libraries have been, fortunately, offering virtual reference services for decades. Thanks to the diverse communication options available on the Internet (e-mail, web forms, social media, etc.), the role of the classic reference desk in the library is more flexible in space and time. This allows librarians to collaborate with patrons at a distance and may substitute for the in-person embedded librarian or liaison librarian. We can see how this was, at least, a path forward toward the MOOC's potential needs.

Some of the MOOC argument comes down to something that is very important in the library training world: information literacy. Does the MOOC topic include the in-depth research and understanding that would encourage a student to explore more resources on this topic? Do they need to know about journals, articles, and databases that could expand their knowledge beyond what the MOOC covers? If they do not have a corresponding assignment, the answer is doubtful. If they do have a corresponding assignment, will the library be able to support these requests?

Public libraries, used to supporting diverse populations across large geographic ranges, may be in better positions to answer MOOC questions, unlike the academic libraries that will, on occasion, restrict help to those affiliated with an academic institution. At academic libraries, many faculty, administrators, and librarians would be hesitant to ask on-campus librarians to support a MOOC that has thousands of participants. Combined with the fact that very few libraries have truly integrated themselves into the MOOC classroom, as they have done with their on-ground counterparts, the thoughts on academic library support for MOOC in this area are limited. However, public libraries, more used to serving the public-at-large, not just the "paying customer," might be able to scale and develop reference and research resources that could speak to some of the information literacy goals.

Preservation, Archiving, and Access

Much like the early Internet pages, and the resulting birth of Internet Archive, someone should take the reins of organizing and preserving MOOC content now, instead of letting it dissolve as classes are re-launched, data is scrubbed, and assets go missing. There is also a question concerning access once a MOOC is "shut off." How do you access version one of the MOOC years later?

Currently, many libraries lack an institutional video platform allowing access to video MOOC content. MOOCs that utilize YouTube and Vimeo to host their content are simply handing content to a third party. Beyond some self-archiving and backup systems, these third parties have no real matching mission or vision to preserve the MOOC institution's scholarly output, whether in the form of videos, quizzes, images, or other content. Here, too, a future role of the library becomes evident: offering corresponding preservation services for MOOC contents as easily as they would other forms of institutional resources.

For some libraries, this new role falls exactly within their current missions: preserve the past versions of MOOCs for future study. As you would imagine, twenty years from now educational scholars will want to see the "origins" of MOOC classes, note how they evolved over time, and actually see, hear, engage, and study MOOC content. It is critical, especially if a library is involved, that steps are taken to preserve all the elements that make up a MOOC.

SAMPLE MOOC STUDIES

We can turn now to brief studies of how libraries and librarians are taking on the roles outlined above. Whether directly involved in MOOC creation, teaching legal research in a MOOC, or providing syllabus support or copyright support, libraries have been revealing their values to the MOOC community in a variety of ways.

Library MOOC Creation

Proving that libraries can create successful MOOCs on their own, Wake Forest University (WFU) librarian Kyle Denlinger built WFU's first information literacy MOOC: "ZSRx: The Cure for the Common Web." Denlinger and the WFU MOOC team offered the course to students, parents, and alumni of WFU. The goal was to allow the community to interact with library staff while also learning more about the web. Since it was limited to WFU students, parents, and alumni, the course attracted less than a full MOOC, but at seven hundred participants, it was still one of the biggest online library courses ever offered.

The class took approximately two hundred hours to create, and Denlinger used free tools, such as Google Sites and Google templates, to fully develop the platform. The lectures were filmed using Denlinger's office web camera. Google Groups and Google+ were harnessed to create the discussion boards and web presence. The course was divided into four modules, which students took at their own pace.

The Google Groups discussions required a good deal of moderation, and Denlinger spent three to four hours moderating, even with the help from two WFU colleagues. Out of 700 participants, 330 people signed up for the Google Group discussions and 50 to 100 participants interacted weekly on the Google+ class blog.

The focus of the class was web literacy. In the WFU community, this topic was well received. WFU community members were accessing the class from all over the world—from students on campus to alumni in Australia. Participants were from twenty-three states and ten countries. However, regardless of this grand international presence, the seven hundred MOOC participants were still small enough to maintain a real community feel—a community, as it turned out, that craved more library classes when he was finished. Three other classes have been launched at WFU since the initial MOOC.

Other libraries have been similarly involved launching their own MOOCs but in a more formal manner, because their university or college had agreed to use an edX or Coursera platform. However, other library systems, such as the New York Public Library (NYPL), have experimented with creating original MOOC content, much like Wake Forest's, but at a public library and without the support of a large, academic, university environment. In 2013, NYPL launched "Sinology 101," a MOOC developed for NYPL by reference librarian Raymond Pun.

NYPL's Schwarzman building features a very famous collection of research and scholarship on Chinese history. Pun, like most librarians looking at the vast treasures in their collections, desired to share that collection with those that would be interested and build community around that collection. Pun accomplished this mission by developing a hybrid course. The MOOC portion of the course was hybridized with an on-ground training on research techniques (you can see some of his presentations on Prezi: "Sinology 101," April 11, 2013, https://prezi.com/). Participants were allowed to concentrate on subjects in Chinese history that were of the most interest to them.

There was no time limit on the learning. The MOOC portion of the class allowed the participants to go at their own learning pace. That way, if they wanted to explore a subject in more detail, they had the time, and the "MOOC clock" was not running on a passing or failing grade. The combination of a hands-on training combined with the sinology MOOC was a success for NYPL.

Teaching Legal Research in MOOCs (University of Florida Levin Law School)

In 2014, University of Florida Levin Law School launched its first law MOOC, "The Global Students Introduction to U.S. Law," through the Coursera platform. In the United States, the legal curriculum typically offers a mandatory basic legal research class in the first year of law school, followed by upper-level advanced research electives later in the curriculum. This class was designed as an introduction for foreign students to learn about the U.S. legal system. The class was taught by eight faculty members at the law school.

Loren Turner, a law librarian, also one of the faculty members teaching the MOOC, was tasked with creating a few modules that would accomplish two learning objectives: (1) introduce MOOC participants to the availability of open-access legal research databases, and (2) demonstrate methods that would increase the participant's own research skills on these databases. While Turner was experienced in teaching legal research in an on-ground capacity, designing the new MOOC legal research course was a new experience. Along with her co-faculty member, and fellow law librarian, Jennifer Wondracek, they set about the task of creating legal research assignments for the MOOC.

The research questions were scheduled to coincide with particular topics. The modules on fundamental liberties, criminal law, and contract law were selected by the faculty to host the research assignment questions. Completion of research assignments were not necessary to complete the class, however; if participants wanted one of Coursera's advanced certificates, they had to complete at least one of the three research assignments. Turner found that the participants that did one assignment were likely to complete the other two as well.

However, before the assignments could be tackled, Turner and Wondracek laid some initial groundwork in the first week by introducing the participants to legal citation, which is necessary for understanding and using the open-access legal databases. In weeks two through seven, the participants had a chance to use the citations in the research questions.

For example, in the criminal law module, Turner introduced a research database. Using a screencast, she showed the participants how to locate an arson statute and a case related to that statute. The screencast allowed the participants to follow along and gain confidence in seeing the instructor perform basic research. Building upon that knowledge, the research question for that week was for the participants to utilize those exhibited skills to find a federal murder statute, which was one of the topics covered by the faculty in the criminal law module for the week.

The research assignments were wildly successful. The course saw more than 2,200 research assignments submitted. But how would you grade such a large amount of research assignments? Turner and Wondracek utilized peer grading for each assignment. They created the following rubric for each participant to use on another participant's answers. The rubric was made as objectively as possible, to allow for simple yes or no answers to be applied simply and efficiently.

- Did your classmate use one (or more) of the following databases for their research (Y/N)?

a. Legal Information Institute (cases and statutes)
b. Google Scholar (cases)
c. FDsys (cases and statutes)
d. CISG Database

- Did your classmate explain how he/she located the case or statute on one of the databases above (Y/N)?
- Did your classmate find a primary legal resource (statute or case) that is relevant to the research topic? (Y/N) Note: If asked to find a case, the case should not be one of those discussed in the class lectures; it should be a new case.
- Did your classmate provide the citation information requested, including the web link to the case or statute? (Y/N)
- Did your classmate summarize the rule of the case or statute? (Y/N)

In teaching the exercises to an international audience, Turner and Wondracek had relatively few problems. However, there were a few instances of access issues that sprung up. For example, a Chinese participant couldn't access Google Scholar to complete an assignment. Turner created a small MOOC video to lead the student to another open-access legal database where he could complete the work. Also, a participant in Germany wasn't seeing the same interface for Google case law. This was a quick fix to the button to access the U.S. Google site, but it was interesting to note that the options were different on research databases around the world.

As far as advice on launching a MOOC with a legal research assignment, Turner suggests starting on the course as early as possible. "It takes longer than you think," she said. Learning Camtasia, going to the video shoot, and scripting the screencast take time.

Fair Use and Copyright Support (Coursera at Duke University)

One of the most famous, yet the least clear, of all the copyright limitations in the Copyright Act, is the doctrine of fair use. Under fair use, you may use copyrighted material without permission from the copyright owner. The doctrine itself was rooted in both English and U.S. case law but was eventually codified in the Copyright Act.

The source of fair-use law is statutory: section 107 of the Copyright Act provides that fair use of a work "for purposes such as criticism, comment, news reporting, teaching (including multiple copies for classroom use), scholarship, or research" is not copyright infringement.[1] This list is not exhaustive; other uses of copyrighted work without permission may also be fair. Section 107 of the Copyright Act provides the following:

> Notwithstanding the provisions of sections 106 and 106A, the fair use of a copyrighted work, including such use by reproduction in copies or phonorecords or by any other means specified by that section, for purposes such as criticism, comment, news reporting, teaching (including multiple copies for classroom use), scholarship, or research, is not an infringement of copyright. In determining whether the use made of a work in any particular case is a fair use the factors to be considered shall include—
>
> 1. the purpose and character of the use, including whether such use is of a commercial nature or is for nonprofit educational purposes;
> 2. the nature of the copyrighted work;
> 3. the amount and substantiality of the portion used in relation to the copyrighted work as a whole; and
> 4. the effect of the use upon the potential market for or value of the copyrighted work.
> 5. The fact that a work is unpublished shall not itself bar a finding of fair use if such finding is made upon consideration of all the above factors.[2]

When the fair-use provision was being proposed, Congress took the position that "since the doctrine is an equitable rule of reason, no generally applicable definition is possible, and each case raising the question must be decided on its own facts."[3] Therefore, when courts are examining a fair-use claim, they analyze each factor using the specific facts of the case to make a fair-use determination. This examination of the four factors determines whether the use is "fair" or constitutes "copyright infringement." Courts weigh each factor and make a decision based on the overview of all four factors.

In the MOOC context, this four-factor test is also used up front for risk mitigation. For example, libraries frequently use this test to determine whether or not they can perform a certain activity or function involving copying or scanning. By reviewing the four factors, as a court might, librarians can determine whether or not the action they are taking might risk infringement or fall squarely within the realm of fair use.

In recent years, U.S. courts have focused increasingly on whether an alleged fair use is "transformative." A work is transformative if, in the words of the Supreme Court, it "adds something new, with a further purpose or different character, altering the first with new expression, meaning or message." Use of a quotation from an earlier work in a critical essay to illustrate the essayist's argument is a classic example of transformative use. A use that supplants or substitutes for the original work is far less likely to be deemed a fair use than one that makes a new contribution.

There are various ways that third-party material—such as a quotation, an image, or a video or music clip—can be used transformatively. For example, it could be the subject of the instructor's analysis. In that case, the material is necessary because the instructor is analyzing, critiquing, or explaining it. Or the material could illustrate the instructor's point or help to make it more comprehensible. Or the material could diagram a process or present a chart or graph of information being discussed by the instructor. These examples are not exhaustive. The key is that the material is being repurposed to significantly advance the instructor's own point.

Transformative use can be contrasted with use that serves more to entertain the audience or to enhance the aesthetics of the presentation. One example of these nontransformative uses is the tangentially related cartoon that enlivens the talk but does little to advance the instructor's argument. Another example is background music. A third example is "set dressing"—the use of background images to improve the visual appeal of the presentation without making a true substantive contribution to the instructor's teaching point. In the practical MOOC world, this is easier said than done. However, one library tackled these copyright, fair use, and licensing problems successfully.

Duke University agreed to start hosting Coursera courses in 2012. As a leader in copyright and scholarly communications under Kevin Smith, director of Copyright and Scholarly Communications, it was natural to see that Duke had decided that a copyright and permissions service should be set up to work with the faculty on the many issues that arise from developing MOOC content. Under Smith's leadership of the Office of Copyright and Scholarly Communication (OCSC), Duke already had a solid reputation among the faculty in helping to advance open access, educating the community about fair use, and creating a shared understanding of aspects of permission and licensing.

Because of the importance of this policy decision, and the potential for a great increase in the workload for the OCSC, a relatively small department in the Duke Library system, Duke's provost provided funding to hire a part-time copyright intern. This intern would work with Smith to help outline the policy for copyright, fair use, and permission with MOOCs at Duke. The policy would serve as an important informational document that faculty members would use to assist with decision making about types of third-party materials in class. Even with the intern, this policy would save the office lots of time, as reviewing third-party materials in each and every MOOC would be overly burdensome for Smith's office, especially in MOOCs where there is a massive reliance on third-party materials.

Duke MOOC instructors were, of course, urged to contact the office with any concerns about a use of copyrighted material. Additionally, when it was determined that permission was needed for a particular use of material, the intern was the point person for contacting and negotiating with publishers, rights holders, and other parties. Another role, besides that of permission, was to find alternate resources and materials that were potentially free of any rights. Obviously an office as steeped in open access and copyright as the OCSC would be best equipped to help instructors find material that was in the public domain, made available through Creative Commons, or generally openly licensed.

Coursera had their own copyright guidelines designed for their instructors. To minimize the risk, these guidelines discouraged the use of third-party copyrighted materials. There is even a section that listed prohibited copyright materials, including anything from Getty Images, popular movies, songs, TV, and famous trademarks.

Duke's copyright guidelines, however, diverged a bit from this template. They did not prohibit instructors from using particular types of content. The rationale was simple: certain classes need access to certain copyrighted material in order to succeed. What would a jazz class be without having some jazz music in it? How could you cover a modern cinema class without some clips from very popular and famous films? Of course, if the music, movie clip, or other third-party copyrighted material is not necessary to the pedagogy of the class, there might be a public domain or Creative Commons–licensed alternative that can be substituted.

Because of the nature of fair use—judged on a case-by-case basis—Duke's guidelines were built to be flexible and the OCSC often provided consultations on specific uses. And on occasion, when the use was determined to be outside the scope of fair use, permission was sought. First, the instructors should provide any identifying information for the content, such as the title, creator, date, URL, and page numbers or time stamps. Secondly, Smith and the OCSC developed a series of questions in order to facilitate effective permission gathering. Each MOOC instructor (and consultants from Duke's Center for Instructional Technology) were asked to answer these questions about the third-party content:

- How do you intend to use the material? (e.g., what lesson you'll be using to teach it, and also if you'll be modifying it, critiquing it, etc.)
- Are you the author/creator of the content?
- Are you willing to provide a link through which students have the option to purchase the material? (Although we avoid requiring any purchases by all students, providing an option to buy an entire book, for example, can increase the rights holders' willingness to allow the use, often without a fee.)
- Will the material be embedded in a video?
- Will the material be included in slides that students can download?
- Would you be willing to link out to the content and then have students restart the lecture from that point after viewing it?[4]

OCSC's guidelines, funding solution, intern program, and copyright and permission expertise, combined with its commitment to support faculty MOOC pedagogy and open access, makes it one of the best examples of library collaboration surrounding one of the most difficult and frustrating aspect of MOOCs: copyright. Their successful story is one that should be emulated by other libraries facing similar issues.

EdX Institutions (HarvardX Syllabus Materials)

In the traditional educational system, the library often serves as the place for course reserves or materials provided to students for their independent use in conjunction with the course. Sometimes these are in print; more recently they are available electronically through content management systems. When we move a course to an online MOOC format, we lose the ability to have a course reserve, whether print or electronic. MOOC participants are not "traditional" students of a college or university and therefore do not have access to the multitudes of subscription databases that could provide these readings. Nor would the MOOC participants be able to access any of the print reserves at the library. MOOC participants can be located anywhere around the world with Internet access. Additionally, the licenses the library has with these databases do not allow the type of distribution necessary to sustain a MOOC. If we started to upload articles, textbooks, or other syllabus materials, we might find ourselves hauled into a court, charged with direct, contributory, or vicarious copyright infringement.

Many institutions have sample guidelines to support both of these types of materials. Here are three strategies for dealing directly with all the problems associated with any syllabus materials. Each has certain advantages and disadvantages but has been used successfully.

Let Their (Student) Fingers Do the Walking

First, if the syllabus material (article or otherwise) is available online, for free, through an open link, then we encourage simply linking to that article. Alternatively, one can simply post the citation to the material with the expectation that participants will acquire it for themselves (by purchasing it, borrowing it from a library, or finding it online). This method has its drawbacks. Frequently, faculty do not have syllabus materials that are open access or linkable. Secondly, many participants (even MOOC participants) expect to be able to acquire the readings, textbooks, or articles for free, or with as little burden as possible. One MOOC, that was cancelled midstream this year, cited the participants' dissatisfaction with the decision to assign a textbook that was not freely available.

Accordingly, if the material is not available via an open link and may be difficult for participants to obtain, we ask the faculty to consider substituting other material that is available, if feasible given the pedagogical aims, or retain a citation to the material but make it *supplemental* rather than required.

The "If You Can't Beat 'Em, Join 'Em"

There is definitely something to be said for making collaborative agreements with major publishers of textbooks or journals for MOOC access. This method has the library reach out to the publishers. Perhaps the faculty only needs a few chapters of a text. Perhaps a "technologically impaired" version can be released. These methods have been successful in the past.

When edX launched "Introduction to Computer Science and Programming" (MITx: 6.00x) taught by Professor John Guttag and others, the MIT Press agreed to provide free access for participants to an online version of the required textbook for the entire duration of the course. This open, online version offered the full text of the book in a static, read-only format. It did not feature all the bells and whistles of a full e-version of the text (e.g., not downloadable for use offline and not searchable), but it still provided the participants with the basic text they would need for the course. To enhance the deal further, MIT Press offered MOOC participants a special price for the print and e-book editions at a 30 percent discount.

The interesting part of this method is that both the publishers and the participants were very pleased with the outcome. From the publisher's side, it increased sales. Even though there was a free static book available, sales of the print and e-book to participants were quite substantial.

Let's Make a Deal

Sometimes, it is best to make a deal before publication. Professor Greg Nagy paid attention carefully when he was signing the contract for his new book *The Ancient Greek Hero in 24 Hours*.

Nagy was converting his course, "The Ancient Greek Hero," which he had taught for thirty-five years at Harvard, to a new online edX module. At the same time, he was in negotiations with Harvard University Press (HUP) for the textbook. He desired the textbook to be free and accessible to the edX participants and wanted the ability to update the text for the class, should he need to for pedagogical reasons.

In a first for both Nagy and HUP, a contract was drawn up that had Nagy forego all his revenue from the sale of the print version of the book to gain an open and free copy of the textbook. The contract gave Nagy the right to make an open-access (OA) copy, in addition to a HTML version for use with his edX course. The HTML copy could be enhanced with multimedia, to enrich the user experience for the participants. And lastly, it gave him the right to post the OA copy to the website of the Center for Hellenic Studies, where Nagy serves as director.

Other faculty heard about this agreement, and as a result, some faculty authors have "gone to the mattresses" for OA access to get similar deals. One current negotiation is between a faculty author creating a MOOC and a major textbook publisher. Reportedly, the faculty member is refusing to sign the publication agreement for the textbook unless it contains similar OA clauses for the edX class access. When the faculty are fully informed of their options and have a clearer understanding of their own publication agreements and the pitfalls, they are more likely to ask for a different agreement, or amend the current agreement.

Conclusion on Syllabus Materials

No school, library, or institution has used only one method for helping with syllabus materials. Some were fortunate enough to have public domain readings available on the Internet Archive or Google Books, some had open-access versions available, and some publishers granted access with no terms but a simple citation requirement. The answers vary as much as the strategies.

Grappling with the syllabus problems for the MOOC courses helped drive a particular mission for librarians to feel very passionate about getting the faculty authors to understand the modern, contract, copyright, and license-bounded world we live in today, and how it affects education. Online classes, like MOOCs, will suffer greatly and will continue to lack the rich and vast resources necessary for true learning if we don't change the nature of where our scholarship ends up or who has access. These strategies were developed as a means of both solving a problem and educating the faculty authors. An opportunity to educate faculty authors about these access issues arises each time a MOOC is proposed and a syllabus or reading list is assembled. Librarians need to be there. It is our job as librarians to "spread the gospel" about copyright, OA, and licensing to make future MOOCs a place where high level of analysis and lecture can be paired with the most interesting and thought-provoking scholarship we have available in the world today.

NOTES

1. 17 U.S.C. §107 (2006).

2. Ibid.

3. H.R. Rep. No. 1476, 94th Cong., 2d Sess. 65 (1976); S. Rep. No. 473, 94th Cong., 1st Sess. 62 (1975), quoted in *American Geophysical Union v. Texaco Inc.*, 37 F.3d 881, 884 (2d Cir. 1994).

4. Lauren Fowler and Kevin Smith, "Drawing the Blueprint as We Build: Setting Up a Library-Based Copyright and Permissions Service for MOOCs," *D-Lib Magazine* 19, nos. 7/8 (2013), http://dx.doi.org/ (featuring the questions and a larger article on the Duke's permissions process).

5

STEP-BY-STEP LIBRARY PROJECTS FOR MOOCS

Creating a massive open online course (MOOC) can be a daunting task. Even with a full understanding of the MOOC pedagogy, the best technical equipment, and a sleek learning management system (LMS) interface, libraries will still need to do some work to get the MOOC content as dynamic and engaging as possible. In this chapter we will learn about the critical planning stages of a library MOOC project and use a few hypotheticals to outline the "how" of using some of the plans and equipment to assemble and launch your MOOC.

PLANNING YOUR FIRST MOOC PROJECT

Now that we have reviewed the policies, tools, applications, and considerations for creating a MOOC, let's review a step-by-step project for a library to plan out a MOOC.

Step 1: Should the Library Create a MOOC?

You have looked at the features of a MOOC and thought it might serve an important purpose at your library or institution. Great! However, you might want to ask these important questions before heading to step 2:

- Could we create a MOOC?
- Should we create a MOOC?
- If we build a MOOC, who would participate?
- How would offering MOOCs serve the library/institutional mission?
- How would offering MOOCs complement, supplement, or compete with our current (or the absence of a current) strategy for online education?

The answers to these questions may alter your strategy on how involved you become with MOOCs at your library or institution. Note that these answers fall across categories such as finance, labor, outreach, technology, and learning. Depending on the initial assessment, some libraries answered these questions and decided to create their own, in-house library MOOC; some did not. If you are in the former category—let's move along to the next important steps.

Step 2: Funding

This is an important step. It is possible to offer a MOOC without significant financial investment (see chapter 3 on the three levels of MOOC finances). If however the MOOC requires something beyond new technology, for example, paid staff to develop and monitor the MOOC, it may be necessary to seek out or budget funding for the development and distribution. Consider reexamining your library budget, and seek grant sources of funding (some are available specifically for MOOC development) or other alternate sources, if necessary.

Step 3: Defining the MOOC Goals/Objectives

This is a large and critical step. Defining goals and objectives of the MOOC up front will definitely affect later important decisions regarding content, video-production style, and financial considerations. The goals for the MOOC should precisely answer the following questions:

- What do you want to achieve?
- What point do you want to reach?

Robert F. Mager, in his book *Preparing Instructional Objectives*, suggests establishing strong learning objectives immediately.[1] Why?

First, when clearly defined objectives are lacking, there is no sound basis for selecting or designing the MOOC's instructional materials, content, or methodologies. This is as true of MOOCs today as it is in the on-ground classroom environment. If you don't know where you are going, it is difficult to select a suitable means for getting there.

Second, establishing strong learning objectives aids the instructor in finding out whether the objective has, in fact, been accomplished. Test or examinations are the indicators for the learning and instruction, and are supposed to inform MOOC instructors and participants whether they have been successful in achieving the course objectives.

Lastly, strong learning objectives provide MOOC participants with a means to organize their own efforts toward accomplishing those objectives. Experience has shown that with clear objectives, participants are better able to decide what activities will help them get to where they decide it is important for them to go in the course.

Step 4: Define the Target Audience

In the last the years, several target audiences have emerged from the MOOC classes. Will one of these target audiences work for your library MOOC? Consider that the library's target audience may impact your marketing, communication, content, and other MOOC considerations.

- Lifelong learners (late and lifelong adult learners)
- Professionals and staff (looking for MOOCs related to professions and work)
- Students (secondary, undergraduate, graduate, etc.)
- Potential undergraduate/graduate students ("testing" classes, both national and international)
- Potential students in secondary education (college prep MOOCs)
- Government

Step 5: Prior Considerations for a MOOC

As we have covered previously, now is the time to make decisions about the following MOOC criteria, which will help with planning the course:

- Course duration (not just "how long is the course" but "can it launch multiple times?")
- Time dedicated to each student (small private online course [SPOC] versus MOOC)
- Student working pace (number of hours per week)
- Content structure
- Learning activities
- Monitoring discussion
- Assessment (quizzes, multiple choice, essay, etc.)
- Deciding on tools for communicating with students (e-mail, social media, blog, etc.)
- Publication time line of the MOOC (week by week, biweekly, monthly, etc.)
- Copyright: resources that are freely accessible versus copyrighted without access

Step 6: Define and Design Content

The MOOC content derives directly from the educational goals (of step 2) and is the basis for learning. Much of this learning will involve the MOOC videos themselves. Once you decide on the duration of the course, you can design a certain number of modules. Each module typically corresponds to one week's worth of learning.

For each module, the major topics, learning outcomes, activities/media to be used, resources, and learner assessments should be specified. The plan will also include sequencing of the modules, course assessment strategy, development process, schedule, and any additional roles and responsibilities.

Each module must have a presentation video, and the lessons should include the following elements:

- Video or videos that show the content of each of the lessons
- Copy of the slides, lessons, scripts, and so forth, in rich text, pdf, or other format
- Weekly readings and resources, if necessary (articles, bogs, other videos, etc.)
- Weekly assessments (quizzes, short essays, etc.)

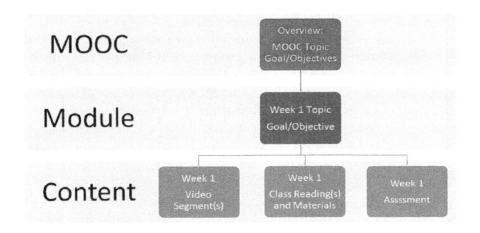

Figure 5.1.

As you sketch out the objective and content for each module, you will see that this will ultimately form the basic structure or skeleton for the course.

Step 7: Select the Form of Assessment Tools

Assessment offers participants the ability to reflect on and understand the processes and concepts that are specific to the MOOC subject. Instructors design activities that give the participants the opportunity to apply the learned content practically, or to offer further teaching points through leading questions and concepts basic on the MOOC assigned videos and readings. Many different types of assessment can be utilized—including multiple-choice quizzes, reading comprehension, and short-answer essays—along with any complementary resources to complete the assessment. Ultimately, the assessment activates basic monitoring and evaluation of the participant's ability to understand the learning objectives.

The assessments should be in line with the teaching content, so that the information supplied is in direct relation to the MOOC learning objectives. MOOC assessments are often accompanied with a corresponding discussion board that opens a forum for dialog postassessment, so that participants may share strategies for good learning practices, problem solving, and time management.

Again, assessments must be designed to measure whether important instructional outcomes have been accomplished. This goal can only be accomplished if the MOOC's instructional outcomes have been made explicit from the very beginning of the MOOC and in each of its corresponding modules. Each type of assessment will benefit a certain subject or topic. While there is a host of ways to assess an individual participant's understanding of the material, a quick review of the most popular would be helpful. The most common assessment tools are as follows:

Quizzes

The quiz method is one of the most basic of MOOC assessments. It offers the instructor an automated system for evaluating many, many participants in a short amount of time. Feedback can be instantaneous. Multiple quizzes can serve as a progress evaluation tool so that participants can test their level of understanding of the content at each module. And if the instructor creates quizzes for each module, it can count toward, or indicate a cumulative end grade for, the course. Types of quizzes include the following:

- Multiple choice
- True or false
- Multiple answer (more than one correct answer)
- Fill in the blank (one or more blanks per question)
- Short answer/short essay
- Math, logic, formula questions

Reading and Discussion Board

MOOCs often feature some outside class reading, which may be critical to the subject. Why not include the reading as part of an assessment? You can assign the readings and ask for a response to each reading on the discussion board. These assessments may result in greater depth of answers and often drum up important and fundamental conversations around the topic. The discussion-board forums can be graded, ungraded, peer graded (see below), or any other combination of assessment. Some MOOC participants have found that much of the learning comes in the form of interactions with the instructors and fellow participants, recreating the "participation" portion of a grade in the typical "in-classroom" environment. While it is not exactly the same as a classroom discussion, it does aid the participant in getting the most out of the MOOC class.

Peer Evaluation

Because of the massive scale of some MOOCs, which can number in the thousands, it would be impossible for an instructor to be able to grade each and every assessment—especially if the assessment is a short answer or mandatory discussion-board post. An instructor can create small peer-to-peer groupings, which in turn can serve as both a grading system and an opportunity for assessment. For example, if you break a class into small groups of three participants each, the assignment is for each participant to read the other two answers and respond. This way each participant submits an answer, gets two forms of feedback, and also, in turn, evaluates two other answers.

The instructor must, of course, give precise instruction on how to evaluate the work of their peers. This is not a dissertation defense, and they are not to attack the peer participant's work. The best practice is for the instructor to create a rubric for grading and commenting on a peer answer. Instructions for these rubrics should be straightforward. Remember, the participant peer graders are just learning about the topic themselves!

Step 8: Detail the Course Plan with a Syllabus

As with an on-campus course, a syllabus might include information from your planning steps above. All you need to do is outline that information in an overall document written for the potential MOOC participant (these are optional, subject to instructor's needs):

- Course name
- List of instructor(s) and any other relevant staff
- Short bio about instructor(s) (recommended: photo)
- Contact information, for individuals, any technology help, and the library
- Topics covered in the course and brief course description
- Course objectives

- Library/institutional logo
- Estimated duration of the course (in weeks)
- Target audience
- Social media profiles on Facebook, Twitter, LinkedIn, or other websites
- Course format, including weekly assignments, final exams, or other assessments
- List of any prerequisites or previous knowledge required
- Recommended reading(s)
- Plagiarism policy or academic integrity statement

Step 9: Create the Videos and Other Content

In this last step you move from planning to action. This will clearly be the most significant portion of time spent on creating the MOOC. Creation of the MOOC videos alone can take hours per module. In the next section we will review some best practices for creating the content of the MOOC videos and consider some of the different styles of MOOC videos. As you are reading the section ask yourself, which style would best serve my library's MOOC?

PLANNING FOR A LIBRARY MOOC VIDEO PROJECT

You have decided to make a MOOC library class. You have created precise learning objectives. You have planned out the topics and the modules, and you have sketched out a draft syllabus with a reasonable time line for the course. You have selected the types of assignments and quizzes you are going to give and have set up basic discussion-board topics. Now it's time to film the crux of any MOOC course: the video. Where do you start? The following are some guidelines for the types of videos, formats, and best practices on developing the most effective MOOC videos for your participants.

Video Lectures: What Type of Lecture Will Serve the Library Best?

There are a wide variety of types of video lectures that an instructor can develop for a MOOC: a video presentation with slides, an in-classroom lecture, a location shoot, a mock interview, and more. But the question that faces many first-time instructors is, what method of video will best serve my MOOC?

A recent study conducted by researchers for edX, "How Video Production Affects Student Engagement: An Empirical Study of MOOC Videos,"[2] examined this exact issue in great detail. Coursera and edX frequently use video lectures as the primary content delivery source. As anyone at these MOOC institutions will tell you, video production is often the highest cost associated with MOOC production, both financial and human. The financial costs can range from a few hundred dollars to the thousands. The "human cost"—time to video, edit, and produce the MOOC segments—can range from an hour per segment to several weeks per MOOC. Instructors need to be able to effectively decide which presentation method works best for their particular MOOC, while still supporting the overall learning goals of the MOOC.

Let us examine some of the results of the 2014 edX report by the authors Philip Guo, Juho Kim, and Rob Rubin, which analyzed MOOC participants' engagement with lecture videos, looking at data gathered from 6.9 million video-watching sessions across four edX courses. This report ultimately revealed some best practices that can aid the success of your MOOC videos.

Examine and Choose the Video Types for the MOOC

MOOC videos are divided into two primary types by the study:

1. Lecture videos for content delivery—presented via an instructor/professor (the "talking head" method); and
2. Tutorial/demonstration, described as a step-by-step, problem-solving module, made popular by the Khan Academy–style online lectures. These are prevalent in computer science courses, mathematical courses, or science courses that feature lab demonstrations.

Video Production Format

The edX report tracked several styles of video production. These are the categories that an instructor might want to consider as part of the MOOC. It is important to note that an instructor does not need to stick to one style of video format. The class topic, learning outcomes, and lesson segments may require you use different styles during different phases of the MOOC.

Lecture-Focused Format

- Lone instructor (no slides): This is the most basic MOOC style, featuring only the instructor (the "talking head" method).
- Instructor with slides: Also basic, with the instructor lecturing, but featuring related PowerPoint presentation slides (or other slide programs). The instructor can appear side by side with the slides, or as a voice-over when he or she is not pictured on screen.
- Classroom lecture: A simple video captured from a live classroom lecture. Note that the edX report strongly recommends against using this style exclusively, as participant engagement was low for these style of MOOC videos.
- Office hours: An instructor filmed as if the participant is meeting and learning in a face-to-face session in his or her office. The instructor speaks directly to the participant. This has the benefit of feeling like a private learning session, where the instructor can present a more casual teaching style, as opposed to a formalized classroom lecture.
- Panel discussion: Many MOOCs have used a panel of topic experts, moderated by the instructor, to serve as focus of the lecture. Occasionally, students are invited to the panel for a similar roundtable discussion of the topic, again, moderated by the instructor.
- In-studio: This more advanced studio shoot features an instructor lecture, often with no audience. Note that this type of lecture, while professionally produced, may be the most expensive option for some MOOC budgets, since a studio shoot requires lighting, cameras, and perhaps even teleprompter technologies.

Tutorial Formats

- Screencast: In these videos, instructors can teach directly off of their computer, capturing the action on their own laptop, as they guide a participant through a lesson.
- Instructor tutorial: A style of video developed and made famous by the Khan Academy online classes, this type of MOOC video features an instructor demonstrating a concept using live pen displays, pen tablets, or styluses. Participants follow along as the instructor draws, calculates, or emphasizes certain subjects. These videos are most popular in MOOC subject categories such as math, computer science, and other sciences.

Which Format to Use?

Now that we have reviewed the many different styles of MOOC video format, the question is, Which style will work best for the MOOC I am creating? Again, it is important to note that an instructor does not need to stick to one style of video format. The class topic, learning outcomes, and lesson segments may require you use different styles during different phases of the MOOC. However, it may be beneficial when creating the first few segments of the MOOC to start with one style of MOOC video.

A second and equally as important question is, What are the human and financial resources available for the MOOC video production? As we saw in chapter 3, there is quite a variety of equipment, hardware, and software that can aid an instructor in creating a MOOC. In addition, you may need additional library staff time to help create the MOOC. That is not to say that a MOOC couldn't be successful on a lower budget. Professor Scott E. Page, of the University of Michigan, recorded a MOOC using a nineteen-dollar camera and a one-hundred-dollar microphone in an unfinished room in his home. The very next year he taped a similar class for the Great Courses series, where the cameras cost $150,000 and a staff of eight helped him with production and editing. Did participants watching the Great Courses learn more than the participants that took the cost-effective MOOC? The answer is no. Budgets can impact video, audio, and other features, but if your topic is engaging, and the instructor's passion comes through, a MOOC can be highly successful on a smaller budget. The participants will learn, and that is the point of the MOOC.

However, the MOOC world has developed some best practices and recommendations that you can follow, regardless of budget, which will make your MOOC more successful. The following are a summary of the seven main findings of the edX study, combined with corresponding recommendations for creators of MOOC videos, provided by Philip Guo, assistant professor of computer science at the University of Rochester:[3]

1. The study revealed that shorter videos are much more engaging. Data indicated that the participant engagement rate drops significantly after six minutes. Guo's recommendation: It is best to invest heavily in preproduction lesson planning to divide videos into smaller segments shorter than six minutes. This, argued Guo, is the most important recommendation of the entire study.

2. Videos that intersperse an instructor's talking head with PowerPoint slides are more engaging than showing only slides. Guo's recommendation: A best practice should be to also invest in postproduction editing to display the instructor's head in some portion of the video. Guo also suggests that a picture-in-picture, featuring both the slides and the instructor's head, might also be beneficial.

3. Videos produced with a more personal feel could be more engaging than high-fidelity studio recordings. Guo's recommendation: Experiment with informal-setting video segments, such as "virtual office hours" or face-to-face tutoring. Guo notes that this style of video is generally a more financially efficient style of filming, with the full benefits of student engagement, and avoids the big budget necessary for studio production.

4. Khan-style tablet drawing tutorials are more engaging than PowerPoint slides or code screencasts. Guo's recommendation: Think about introducing motion and "visual flow" into the tutorials. Combining this with an active voice-over from the instructor, MOOC participants can follow along with the instructor's thought process.

5. Even high-quality, prerecorded classroom lectures are not as engaging when chopped up into short segments for a MOOC. Guo's

recommendation: The classroom lecture format does not translate well in the MOOC environment. If possible, the instructor should plan to make the classroom instruction amenable to the technologically rich MOOC environment through careful lesson planning, which will ensure a better level of participant engagement. Perhaps reach out to those with expertise in the online learning environment.

6. Videos where instructors speak fairly fast and with high enthusiasm are more engaging. Guo's recommendation: Not surprisingly, instructors with a real passion and enthusiasm for the topic do very well with high participant engagement, even if they are talking at a quick pace. Don't slow down the passionate instructor, Guo says; MOOC participants always have the ability to stop the video if they want a break, or need to hear a part of the lecture again.

7. Students engage differently with lecture and tutorial videos. Guo's recommendation: Tutorial videos and lecture videos should each feature a different focus. Tutorial videos may require more support for rewatching or skimming—going back over a concept or labeling a concept clearly in the video. Lecture videos should focus more on what Guo calls "the first-time watching experience."

More Tools for a Successful MOOC Shoot

By now you have selected the type of MOOC videos you are going to produce. You have outlined several smaller video segments to be part of each week's module. You are ready to move into production of these videos. What are the next few things you may need to create a successful MOOC video shoot?

MOOC Script

A script can help you flesh out all the information and learning outcomes you want to have in each module, each week. Without a script, an instructor may be lost as to what topics will be covered in which segment, and when. Now, some MOOCs are scripted, and some are not. Some are merely outlined and allow the instructor to improvise and mimic the classroom environment. But there are several advantages to writing a script out: it can help you express exactly what is going to go in each video segment; it can be shared with others on your MOOC team to help improve the language or pedagogy; and it will serve as an annotated table of contents for your course—clearly outlining the sequence of each learning module's focus. For most MOOC instructors, even if you have been teaching for years, this may be your first scripting attempt. Treat it exactly as you imagine a Hollywood producer would—give your MOOC the structure it needs. Each script for each video module basically needs the following: (1) a welcome/introduction, (2) content and lessons, (3) a preview of topics to come (optional), and (4) an exit. If you stick to the MOOC best practices, each video segment can be in the seven- to ten-minute range, which, with certain topics, can be easily scripted.

Example

Intro screen with library logo and title of course
Chris Smith: "Welcome to Library MOOC. My name is Chris Smith, and I will be your guide over the next few weeks, as we explore the library's unique collection and . . ."
Content and Lessons: Research Databases
Research Exercise—Short Quiz
Exit: "I hope you enjoyed our first session of Library MOOC. Next time we will explore the library's historical archives. See you next week!"
Outro screen with library logo and title of course

There is a lot more work than our basic example above, but once you start to write, using the syllabus and the course plan as your guide, you will find it becomes easier to script each module and segment.

One important key to this equation is practice. No one acts exactly the same on camera as they do in real life. The camera adds an element that you can't foresee. You can get over any fears by continually practicing what you've scripted. Read it out loud to yourself. Read it to your colleagues. Does it sound natural? Does it seem relaxed and easy? Do the points and sequence of dialog make sense? Practice will help you with the editing process and make your MOOC sound and look more professional.

MOOC Storyboard

Now that you have a script, what might be another tool to aid the overall quality of the MOOC? While many MOOC instructors can work solely off a script, notes, or improvisational talks, there are great benefits to outlining the MOOC in a storyboard. Storyboards use images and written instructions to plan your MOOC course, including the sequence of events. Basic storyboards look like a small comic strip of your MOOC and are critical to MOOCs using more than one style of video shooting that necessitates a step-by-step layout of the video's content.

Using the images, shots, and sequences in a storyboard can help truly visualize the larger goals of the MOOC and can create a greater learning experience for both the participant and the instructor. Many participants in your MOOC will value the sequential learning patterns designed in the storyboard, as they become "real" when you start to film them on video. By having a step-by-step visual plan, every person involved, regardless of their role, can see exactly what the finished product will look like and contribute suggestions.

Figure 5.2 shows a standard storyboard template, filled in with the notes of a hypothetical MOOC production.

Instead of drawing each module storyboard by hand, you might consider some digital tools. One online service for storyboarding is called Storyboard That (http://www.storyboardthat.com/), which offers a host of designs, templates, and storyboard options for a quick and efficient process. You can use the free storyboard version, or it is reasonably inexpensive to sign up for the full version, should you consider storyboarding more MOOC classes in your future.

MOOC Filming Location

Hopefully your MOOC plan, script, and storyboard identified places you want to film your MOOC. MOOCs have been filmed in offices, classrooms, laboratories, libraries, and other more exotic locations, should the topic call for it. For some, MOOCs location is about telling a particular story—for example, shooting at historic sites in Greece for a MOOC on the legends of Greek heroes. For others, MOOCs location is about finding a quiet, well-lighted, and secluded place to teach without interruption.

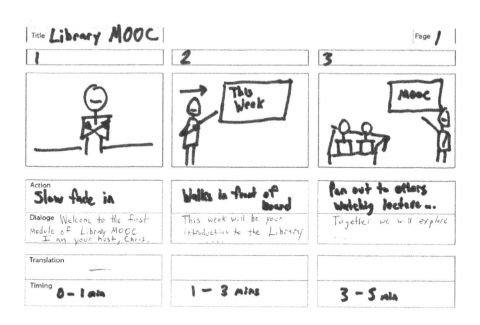

Title **Library MOOC**   Page **1**

1	2	3

Action

1. Slow fade in
2. Walks in front of board
3. Pan out to others watching lecture...

Dialoge

1. Welcome to the first Module of Library MOOC. I am your host, Chris.
2. This week will be your introduction to the Library...
3. Together we will explore...

Translation

Timing

1. 0 – 1 min
2. 1 – 3 mins
3. 3 – 5 min

Figure 5.2. A very basic MOOC storyboard

When you are creating your first library MOOC, it would make sense for your library to appear front and center. Even if you opt for a basic MOOC screencast, only viewing the instructors as they emphasize lessons on their computer, a background that includes some of the library (stacks, reference desks, common rooms, etc.) will go far to set the character of the MOOC. Perhaps you can even dedicate a few shots for the introduction in the library stacks, before moving to a quiet, well-lighted office for the majority of the MOOC video.

Regardless of what location you choose, make sure to scout it out in advance. How does it look during the day, in the afternoon, or at night? Will you require more lighting in a particular space, or will you need to block out the office windows because they are too bright? Sound is also a serious issue. For the clarity of instructions, and to aid the use of your built-in or external microphone, you need to know how much ambient noise is being picked up on the mics in a particular location. As any librarian can testify, sometimes the library is not the quietest of spaces. Think of filming before or after closing time. Or if the segment calls for it, shoot the library during high-traffic time, so the world can see how busy your library can get. Lastly, check the power options available at each location. Are there enough plugs? Do you need to bring extension cords or surge protectors? Do you need to bring batteries because of the lack of plugs? All of these questions can be answered with a basic location scouting trip.

HOW TO CREATE MOOCS FOR BIBLIOGRAPHIC INSTRUCTION

In this section, we will put it all together—the educational goals, plans, syllabus, video choices, editing choices, and the technology and equipment necessary—into one process for creating a library MOOC. In this hypothetical project we will be designing a library MOOC for a general bibliographic instruction class, on a library research catalog named "KatLib." Before we dig into the MOOC further, let us explore a basic summary that can be used for all MOOCs and that takes into account nearly all the factors and decisions surrounding a MOOC. This "cheat sheet," titled the "MOOC Appraisal Sheet," will serve as the outline for all of our MOOCs, as we answer the questions briefly under each category.

Now let's apply the questions from the MOOC appraisal sheet to our MOOC bibliographic instruction class on KatLib.

Note: This hypothetical includes various options for PC and Mac technology. As this is a proposed project, many of the technologies from chapter 3 can serve as a substitute for the specifics listed below. I have used specifics here to reveal how the choices of technology and strategy are blended into a final MOOC project.

Q1.1. What Human Resources Do You Have Available to Dedicate toward Creating This MOOC?

This MOOC will be created with the help of the three librarians from the state library who will serve as the co-instructors for the class, one from reference, one from circulation, and one from technical services. The library estimates thirty hours of total staff time to develop approximately four hours of MOOC content and assessment.

MOOC Appraisal Sheet

1. People	Q1.1. What human resources do you have available to dedicate toward creating this MOOC? Q1.2. Do you need to hire outside the library to help run the MOOC?
2. Resources	Q2.1. What learning materials, open educational resources, videos, slides, and so forth, do you already have for launching the MOOC? Q2.2. Do you need to purchase more educational resources for the MOOC?
3. Equipment	Q3.1. What hardware do you have in order to create the MOOC content? Q3.2. What software do you have in order to create the MOOC content? Q3.3. What additional hardware/software do you need to purchase to create the MOOC content?
4. Platform	Q4.1. What type of formats are supported on your platform? Q4.2. What type of assessments are supported on your platform?
5. MOOC description	Q5.1. What is the name of your MOOC? Q5.2. What is the duration of your MOOC (weeks)? Q5.3. What is the topic of your MOOC?
6. Target audience	Q6.1. What is the target country, state, or town for your MOOC? Q6.2. What is the level of education necessary to take your MOOC?
7. Objectives/goals	Q7.1. What are the learning objectives of the MOOC? Q7.2. What competencies will participants acquire in the MOOC?
8. MOOC contents	Q8.1. What is the structure of the MOOC? Q8.2. What format(s) will you utilize for your MOOC contents?
9. Assessment	Q9.1. What type of weekly assessment will the MOOC utilize? Q9.2. What type of final assessment will the MOOC utilize?
10. Other Media and Technology	Q10.1. Will you use additional media for advertising, promotion, discussion, and so forth?

Q1.2. Do You Need to Hire outside the Library to Help Run the MOOC?

In this scenario, the library does not foresee any additional hiring necessary.

Q2.1. What Learning Materials, Open Educational Resources, Videos, Slides, and So Forth, Do You Already Have for Launching the MOOC?

KatLib is the enhanced library catalog in the state library, and as a result, there are plenty of resources such as slides, handouts, and training exercises that have been previously offered in on-ground classes. Additionally, since KatLib is part of a greater library catalog system that other academic libraries in the state also use, the library can draw upon other resources for research instruction.

Q2.2. Do You Need to Purchase More Educational Resources for the MOOC?

The library does not need to purchase any additional educational resources.

Q3.1. What Hardware Do You Have in Order to Create the MOOC Content?

Many libraries feature either Windows-based or Mac-based computers. Here we will describe two hypothetical options. Note that whether you have a Mac or a PC, you can definitely create and launch a MOOC similar to this project.

Option 1   Windows PC: The library has a Dell Latitude Ultrabook E7240 with 16 GB RAM and a 250 GB hard drive. Camera: The Dell has a built-in Integrated HD Webcam, which the library will use for recording.

Option 2   Mac Computer: The library has a Mac Pro (OSX) with 16 GB RAM and a 500 GB hard drive. Camera: The Mac Pro has a built-in iSight HD camera, which the library will use for recording

Q3.2. What Software Do You Have in Order to Create the MOOC Content?

Option 1   Windows Screen Capture: SnagIt. The library will use SnagIt's free, fifteen-day trial to screen capture. With the recording features, the library can screencast the video lecture and include on-screen brief tutorials that demonstrate the KatLib.

Option 1   Windows Video Editing Software: Windows Movie Maker. The Dell laptop can easily download and run Windows Movie Maker to make the edits to the captured video.

Option 2   Mac Screen Capture: QuickTime X. The Mac Pro the library owns has QuickTime X, the media player for Mac OS X. With the recording features, the library can screencast the video lecture and include on-screen brief tutorials that demonstrate the KatLib. (The library also has a Mac version of PowerPoint available, which can record audio with each slide for a complete presentation.)

Option 2   Mac Video Editing Software: iMovie. The software iMovie comes with each Mac and is very easy to use. The library can easily import the recorded QuickTime MOOC videos and edit.

Q3.3. What Additional Hardware/Software Do You Need to Purchase to Create the MOOC Content?

Platform Option 1   No platform. The library will use YouTube and Google Groups to mimic a MOOC platform. While YouTube will simply host the videos, there is still a need for discussion and assessment. We will use a library-created Google Groups site for this type of necessary MOOC interaction.

Platform Option 2   LearnDash. LearnDash is a supplemental WordPress MOOC platform add-on. It is easy to install, learn, and implement. The benefit is that the library already has a WordPress account for its blog, and the instructors are familiar with the system.

Q4.1. What Type of Formats Are Supported on Your Platform?

Option 1   YouTube supports video. Google Groups supports the discussion.

Option 2   LearnDash, via WordPress, allows the library to upload text, Word docs, pdf files, and embedded media from YouTube, Vimeo, or other video media sites. It also includes MOOC features for ready-made quizzes, discussion boards, and short-answer questions.

Q4.2. What Type of Assessments Are Supported on Your Platform?

Option 1   Google Groups supports basic group discussion and the potential for short-answer questions using peer-grading. The library

KatLib MOOC under this option will have basic discussion and short answers.

Option 2 LearnDash supports almost every type of assessment including multiple choice, multiple answer, short answer, fill in the blank, discussion-board assignments, and more. The library KatLib MOOC under this option will utilize a combination of multiple-choice quizzes, short answer, and the discussion-board posts.

Q5.1. What Is the Name of Your MOOC?

KatLib MOOC

Q5.2. What Is the Duration of Your MOOC (Weeks)?

Four weeks.

Q5.3. What Is the Topic of Your MOOC?

Library research using KatLib.

Q6.1. What Is the Target Country, State, or Town for Your MOOC?

KatLib MOOC is a fully open MOOC to the Internet. However, participants in the state, using KatLib at the state library, would benefit the most. Others may also be interested in the general information and research tips.

Q6.2. What Is the Level of Education Necessary to Take Your MOOC?

No particular level required.

Q7.1. What Are the Learning Objectives of the MOOC?

1. Locate and learn the basic use of KatLib, both on the Internet and on the KatLib mobile version.
2. Choose the right key words to find books, articles, and other resources in KatLib.
3. Learn advanced KatLib searching with subject, author, title, and WorldCat.
4. Learn the procedure for ordering books from other libraries through KatLib.

Q7.2. What Competencies Will Participants Acquire in the MOOC?

1. Applied learning—successfully utilizes new KatLib knowledge, understanding, and skill in an educational environment
2. Maximize learning—participates in MOOC learning activities, making the most of the learning experience
3. Scheduling—effectively allocates own time to complete MOOC work

Q8.1. What Is the Structure of the MOOC?

Five modules with content, instruction, and assessment.

Q8.2. What Format(s) Will You Utilize for Your MOOC Contents?

Screencast videos, pdf handouts, PowerPoint, or other media (as appropriate).

Q9.1. What Type of Weekly Assessment Will the MOOC Utilize?

Depending on the platform options above, it will feature multiple-choice quizzes, short answers, or discussion-board posts.

Q9.2. What Type of Final Assessment Will the MOOC Utilize?

The final assessment will be a hypothetical start-to-finish research process, using KatLib, which will illustrate the participant's new KatLib knowledge. Participants will post an annotated research "pathfinder" logging the successful (and unsuccessful) searches and resources found for the topic they are assigned.

Q10.1. Will You Use Additional Media for Advertising, Promotion, Discussion, and So Forth?

Facebook, Twitter, and the library's blog and web page.

Now we have the basic formula from the MOOC appraisal sheet for the library MOOC. Let's revisit scripting. For this MOOC project, the library is doing a screencast. A screencast is typically a different type of MOOC, in that you will see less of the instructor and more of the instructor's computer screen. In the KatLib MOOC, participants will be looking at KatLib quite a bit. As a result, the script for a MOOC screencast needs to be slightly different. Take a look at the following guidelines for MOOC screencast scripts.

Writing a Script for a MOOC Screencast

- For formal videos demonstrating precise instructions, write a word-for-word script.
- Develop a screencast script template. Since KatLib MOOC is featuring three different instructors, uniformity in the design and layout of the scripts is as important as uniformity in the videos themselves.
- Each instructor should use a standard welcome/introduction and a standard conclusion for further uniformity.
- Take screenshots as the script develops. You can easily note in the script the precise screenshot that matches the narration in the video. It will be easier, then, to illustrate that action as you are speaking and lecturing. In effect, you will be walking through the same shoes as your participants, methodically going through the functions and features of the KatLib MOOC participants.
- Talk as if you were explaining the MOOC concept on an elevator. It makes the tone conversational and more likely to engage the participant.
- MOOC instructors have employed speech-recognition programs (such as Dragon Naturally Speaking) while they are running through the MOOC lecture to help develop the screencast script automatically.
- As you write and edit the script, read it out loud. Do you sound natural? Is the sentence too long? This also helps you write transitions between actions.
- Always provide context. Clearly explain "the why" to the participants as they will be following along through the KatLib MOOC.
- Narration should be straightforward and to the point.
- Save any assets (scripts, screenshots, notes, and other files) as you are developing the script. Always employ a NASA-like triple backup, so that if you lose the original script, you can rebuild it simply and efficiently.

You have your script and corresponding screenshot action. Now it's time to record. Since we will be using a mix of PowerPoints for slides and QuickTime for screencasts, let's look at the basic functions of both these options as the library would prepare to record the KatLib MOOC.

Basic PowerPoint or QuickTime Screencast with Audio

A screencast will be one of the best tools to use for this particular MOOC. The library instructor must to be able to display the KatLib catalog in order to show its many new features that will benefit both patrons and librarians. A screencast does not necessarily mean that you have to run out and spend lots of money on equipment. For this bibliographic instruction MOOC, we can again take a cue from Professor Scott E. Page, of the University of Michigan, and instructor of the Coursera "Model Thinking" MOOC. He launched a "garage band version" of his course that was very popular and was recorded simply using a nineteen-dollar camera and a one-hundred-dollar microphone in an unfinished room in his home.

Many libraries have PowerPoint (PC or Mac) or QuickTime (PC or Mac) already loaded into the computers. Whether it's a desktop or a laptop, these programs do feature some very basic screencasting audio and video functions that can help with the MOOC content creation process. Let's examine both PowerPoint and QuickTime as two options for our screencast portion of our KatLib MOOC.

First Step: Setting the Audio for a Screencast

Before you record audio for the slideshow, your computer must be equipped with a microphone. As noted, many basic webcams or USB microphones are available for a low cost. Additionally, you should consider monitoring your recording with a pair of headphones. These will also come in handy when you edit your video. Most video professionals recommend over-ear headphones (see chapter 3 for further recommendations).

Depending on the microphone used, you might need to adjust the location of the microphone. If we are using the Blue Snowball mic, recommended in chapter 3, we should set the mic up about one foot from your face. With the headphones on, you will notice if it's too close (audible feedback and other noise) or too far away (too quiet or subdued sound). Again, the space in which you record will remain a major factor in how the final audio and video recording will translate to the MOOC. If you record in a small room, you might avoid the echo of the lecture hall or the background noise of the library. Even a small group-study room might be better than a classroom environment or an office with many windows. Test the microphone and adjust any audio levels so that your normal speech volume will be enough for the recording, and hit the "sweet spot" of audio clarity.

Second Step (Option 1): Recording Narration in a PowerPoint Slideshow

You can either record audio before you run a slideshow or record a narration during a slideshow. If you want the video to only have narration where necessary, you also have the option to record audio on selected slides. As soon as you add audio to a slide, a sound icon appears on the slide. As with any sound in PowerPoint, you have the option to click on the icon and play the audio, or set it to play automatically.

Before you start recording, PowerPoint 2010 will prompt you to record just the slide timings, just the narrations, or both at the same time. You can set the slide timings manually so that you can give a scripted lecture as the slides progress forward. This is another way of staying within the recommended time limits for full participant engagement in video segments for a MOOC. Set the slideshow to seven to ten minutes, and try to stay within that time frame. Remember, recording slide timings will also record the times of animations or scrolling text.

Record a Narration Before or During a Slideshow

Step 1: When you record a narration, you run through the presentation and record each slide. You can pause and resume recording any time.

Step 2: Ensure your microphone is set up and in working order prior to recording your slideshow.

Step 3: On the Slide Show tab, in the Set Up group, click Record Slide Show.

Step 4: Select one of the following: start recording from beginning or start recording from current slide

Step 5: In the Record Slide Show dialog box, select the Narrations and laser pointer check box and, if appropriate, select or deselect the Slide and animation timings check box.

Step 6: Click Start Recording.

Step 7: To end your slideshow recording, right click the slide and then click End Show.

Step 8: The recorded slideshow timings are automatically saved, and the slideshow appears in Slide Sorter view with timings beneath each slide.

Record Comments on a Slide

Step 1: In Normal view, click the slide that you want to add a comment to.

Step 2: On the Insert tab, in the Media group, click the arrow under Audio and then click Record Audio.

Step 3: To record the comment, click Record, and start speaking.

Step 4: When you are finished recording, click Stop.

Step 5: In the Name box, type a name for the sound and then click OK. A sound icon appears on the slide.

Second Step (Option 2): Recording Narration in QuickTime

You can use QuickTime X to record everything that happens on your computer's screen or on a portion of your computer's screen, along with your narration, if you'd like. This is called a screen recording. (Note: The Windows version of QuickTime does not currently allow screen recording; only the Mac version has this important feature.) It is one of the simplest processes for recording.

Go to the menu bar, and select Choose File; then, in the dropdown, New Screen Recording. To start recording what's occurring on your Mac's screen, click the round record button.

You can record all or some of the screen, depending on the instructor's plan. If you want to record the entire screen, click anywhere on the screen to start recording. To record just a smaller portion of the screen, drag your pointer to select the region of the screen you want to record and then click the Start Recording button within the region. To stop recording, click the stop button in the menu bar.

Clicking the triangle in this window gives you additional options, such as letting you choose whether to use the built-in microphone on your Mac, the connected Snowball microphone, or if the lesson requires no sound but simple "follow-along" images, no microphone at all.

This same menu also lets the instructor select whether or not your mouse clicks are shown during the recording.

Third Step: Import to Video Editor and Edit

Once you have filmed the screencasts, you then can edit the clips in a video-editing software program. At this point the instructors will have the ability to decide about a lot of editing and polishing effects, including transitions, screen wipes, standardized introductions, logos, and other special effects. If your library is using a PC, the Windows Movie Maker has one of the simplest drag-and-drop editing interfaces. If you are using a Mac, when you import your QuickTime videos for editing, iMovie automatically loads the videos into its interface for simple editing.

As described in chapter 3's review, both Windows Movie Maker and iMovie employ very simple drag-and-drop interfaces working inside the video time line. The learning curve for iMovie or Windows Movie Maker are not nearly as high as their more expensive cousins, Adobe Premiere and Final Cut Pro X, but there are plenty of manuals, tutorials, and videos out there for instructors to master any program's features in no time.

Tips on Screencasts

KatLib MOOC will only feature the basic screencasts recorded and edited with a basic video editor such as Windows Movie Maker or iMovie. The basic MOOC model for this type of video style should employ some of the best practices developed to maintain the participant's interest and dedication to the MOOC. These best practices are not just from the MOOC arena but are developed over time with the rise of online learning over twenty years ago. Many of these recommendations are similar to the recommendations for an effective video shoot (scripting, practice, etc.), but it is critically important to reemphasize them here because of the nature of the screencast.

- Clearly define the topic and learning objectives for your screencast upfront. Give students an "advance organizer" of some sort (e.g., outline or concept map) that will give students a good idea of where the presentation is going.

- Don't wait until the last minute; it will take you longer than you think, especially in the beginning.
- Speak slowly.
- Let the video do the talking. Show the steps, and talk about the importance of the process that you're demonstrating. You do not need to talk about every detail; there is a strong visual element.
- Use the best audio you can, and test your audio equipment frequently.
- Record in a quiet location.
- Use "special effects" and "clever transitions" sparingly.
- Clean up a cluttered or busy desktop. The participants are going to be looking directly at your computer screen for the majority of the class.
- Control your mouse movements by using slow movements across the screen.
- Be yourself, and share your passion for the topic.

Basic Elements of the KatLib MOOC

Each MOOC, including the library's, has a unique set of elements that need to be developed and deployed. Let's examine the backbone of the library MOOC's content.

1. KatLib lectures—Five modules with content, instruction, and assessment, hosted on YouTube, and imported to WordPress LearnDash.
2. Weekly reading assignments—pdf handouts summarizing and expanding on the lesson for each week.
3. Weekly problems—These will feature in-depth problems testing the core learning objectives:

    a. Locate and learn basic use of KatLib, both on the Internet and the KatLib mobile version (multiple choice)
    b. Choose the right key words to find books, articles, and other resources in KatLib (multiple choice)
    c. Learn advanced KatLib searching with subject, author, title, and WorldCat (short answer)

    d. Learn the procedure for ordering resources from other libraries through KatLib (short answer)

4. Final exam—The final assessment will be a hypothetical start-to-finish research process, using KatLib, which will illustrate the participant's new KatLib knowledge and skills. Participants will post an annotated research "pathfinder" logging the successful (and unsuccessful) searches and resources found for the topic they are assigned on the discussion board. Participants will then get to share and comment upon other topics and pathfinders in the course.

Making a library research assignment for a MOOC is a little different than making a research assignment for a classroom or library environment. For the advanced searching for weekly problems and the final exam, there are some recommendations to keep in mind when developing the KatLib MOOC research assignments:

- Address the learning outcomes related to the research process. Consider what research skills you would like the participants to develop on completing the assignments. During the lecture, you can even discuss with your students the importance of developing those skills in KatLib.
- Clearly define your expectations for the assignment. The KatLib MOOC will be made up of people who may not have prior experience with libraries, research, resources, and of course KatLib— that is why they are taking the class. The more you define the why of the assignment, related to one of the core learning objectives, the more the participant will understand the purpose and practice involved in completing an assignment.
- Break larger assignments into smaller, sequential research tasks. Just like the recommendation for shorter video lengths in a MOOC, you can break a large research assignment into several parts. It may be only three questions, but it has several subheadings that relate to a research step or concept. Participants will learn to focus on particular skills to develop, and see the big picture in the research process.
- Create a "Questions for the Instructors" discussion board. During the course, you may receive several questions about the research

assignments from participants that are virtually the same. Instead of replying with the same answer each time, you can post one response to a general forum, and everyone can then see your reply.

- Use discussion boards also for assignment wrap-up. Make a space on the discussion boards for participants to reflect on the research assignments. Not only will it encourage further conversation and questions, much as an in-classroom discussion, but also it gives the instructor the opportunity to weigh in on the importance of the research assignment. KatLib participants will want to hear what the instructor stressed as important about the research question for that week.

- Clarify the grading process. In the written instructions for the assignment, make it clear how the research assignment will be graded, and define the particular expectations for completion. The KatLib MOOC participants can't drop by for office hours to see you explain something in person. They only have the videos and the assignment instructions. If necessary, record a small video supplement to clarify.

- Road test your own assignment (colleagues too). Take the time to do the research assignment you will release to the participants. Testing the assignment will uncover any missing parts of the question, technical obstructions, or problems with the description of the research questions. If you have the time, make some colleagues run through the KatLib assignments as well. Outside opinions can really clarify what may be lacking.

Launching the Class

The day is finally here. You have planned, scripted, taped, edited, written, uploaded to YouTube, and prepped everything for launch in your choice of MOOC platform—whether you are using WordPress's LearnDash, Blackboard's CourseSites, or some combination of YouTube video hosting and Google Groups discussion board. Now's the exciting part—launch the course! However, here are a few tips for you to consider while your MOOC is running:

- Provide feedback and be active and busy during the course. Studies have indicated that the more an instructor interacts with a MOOC, the more the participants stay interested and engaged.
- Use social media channels. After launch, consider using Twitter, Facebook, a blog, or other methods to send out short communications or teasers about the week ahead. Maybe even have a Twitter hashtag #KatLibMOOC. Participants are not obligated to use these platforms, but many will, sometimes just to interact with each other, or create their own online learning communities outside the MOOC.
- Provide support and moderation. MOOC participants will expect you to "have the answers" when it comes to technical questions, policy questions, and a host of other questions. Be prepared, especially in the first week.
- Avoid changing the course midcourse, and maintain deadlines. Since this is the first iteration (and hopefully one of many) of KatLib MOOC, allow the course to run without changes, so you have a clear understanding of what might need to change next time. Changing assignments, dates, and other deadlines may lead to class-wide confusion.
- Send a welcome message at the beginning of each week and a wrap-up message at the end of the week. It would be really helpful to provide a brief overview to the participants of what they will experience and what they can be prepared for. When the week concludes, send a concluding message emphasizing the main points of the week, and give a review of the overall effort.
- End-of-course surveys. Want to get some additional feedback? Simply use Survey Monkey, or other basic, free Internet polling software, to develop a MOOC "exit interview." Find out what participants liked, didn't like, or what they might change. Listen to your course participants; they will freely tell you what to improve.

HOW TO CREATE MOOCS FOR STAFF TRAINING: ADVANCED SPOC PROJECT

Let's continue to use some of the knowledge we have from previous chapters and projects to create an advanced library MOOC for staff training. This will be different from the KatLib MOOC we previously discussed and outlined. Internal staff trainings are less like a fully open MOOC, and more like the limited SPOC class, where the class size is restricted to participants that are staff members of the library. In this case we will be teaching a small course on our new internal reference and research tracking program, called TrackRef, being adopted across all the libraries in the academic consortium.

Note: This advanced SPOC hypothetical includes various options for PC and Mac technology. As this is a proposed project, many of the technologies from chapter 3 can serve as a substitute for the specifics listed below. I have used specifics here to reveal how the choices of technology and strategy are blended into the final green-screen SPOC project.

On Renting Equipment

Much like many of the thirty-day trials recommended in chapter 3, there are always alternate options to paying for a product or technology. This proposed advanced SPOC project may come with a higher price; however, there is always an option to rent the equipment outlined in this section. Many MOOCs and SPOCs have been created with equipment rented from programs such as Borrow Lenses (http://www.borrowlenses.com/) or ATS Rentals (http://www.atsrentals.com/). Renting from either of these companies can ensure a low cost and also gives the library staff the unique opportunity to practice with the advanced equipment.

Again, let us go through the relevant questions from the MOOC appraisal sheet, and address the specifics of this more advanced SPOC production.

Q1.1. What human resources do you have Available to dedicate toward creating this MOOC?

This SPOC will be created with the help of the three reference staff members at the main library, who will serve as co-instructors for the class; one IT worker to aid with the hardware/software; and some of the circulation staff (when available). The library sees about ten hours of staff time to develop approximately 1.5 hours of SPOC content and assessment.

Q1.2. Do You Need to Hire outside the Library to Help Run the MOOC?

In this scenario, the library does not foresee any additional hiring necessary.

Q2.1. What Learning Materials, Open Educational Resources, Videos, Slides, and So Forth, Do You Already Have for Launching the MOOC?

Since the TrackRef is relatively new to the library, we will be developing the learning materials and videos in-house. TrackRef did, however, give us a set of PowerPoint slides for their basic training, which we will incorporate into out materials. Permission has been granted to use this PowerPoint presentation.

Q2.2. Do You Need to Purchase More Educational Resources for the MOOC?

The library does not need to purchase any additional educational resources.

Q3.1. What Hardware Do You Have in Order to Create the MOOC Content?

Option 1   Windows PC: The library can use something basic such as a Dell Latitude Ultrabook E7240 with 16 GB RAM and a 250 GB hard drive. Camera: The Dell has a built-in Integrated HD Webcam, which the library will use for recording.

Option 2   Mac Computer: Or, on the Mac side, the library can use something similarly basic such as a Mac Pro (OSX) with 16 GB RAM and a 1 TB external hard drive for storage. Camera: The Mac Pro has a built-in iSight HD camera, which the library will use for recording. Audio: The library has, purchased for other events and teaching, a Zoom H4 audio recorder with a lapel mic. This setup will create more quality audio for the MOOC, since the built-in camera and the external camera have nonadjustable microphones.

Q3.2. What Software Do You Have in Order to Create the MOOC Content?

Option 1   Windows Screen Capture: QuickTime Player. The Mac Pro comes with QuickTime, the default media player for Mac OS X. With the recording features, the library can supplement the video lecture with brief tutorials that demonstrate the basics of TrackRef.

Option 2   PC Screen Capture: Screencast-O-Matic. This basic software package allows a free and easy interface to record what's on the instructor's screen and can easily be combined with the main camera's green-screen recording. The basic version is free and very simple to use. Videos in the free version are limited to fifteen minutes.

Q3.3. What Additional Hardware/Software Do You Need to Purchase to Create the MOOC Content?

Video Camera (and Tripod)   Video cameras, in this case, will be used to tape the main green-screen portion of the SPOC and feature a great range of pricing options. See chapter 3 for a review of many types of camera options. For example, on the high end would be a Nikon D7000 16.2 Megapixel Digital SLR Camera with 18–105 mm lens. While the library can consider cheaper video cameras, the DSLR prices have come down (six-hundred-dollar range) to make it a worthwhile investment for some libraries. A cheaper (but still reasonably priced) video camera could be easily substituted here. For example, a Panasonic HC-V550K HD is a solid video camera for the SPOC's purpose. It has solid HD memory and a long zoom lens. An even lower priced option could be the Flip UltraHD Video Camera, as reviewed in chapter 3. This camera allows basic "shoot and share" in superior HD. Regardless of the camera ultimately purchased, the library should also have a tripod capable of handling the weight of any of the cameras. On the high end, some DSLRs come with a remote control that allows the instructor to activate the camera remotely (SSE's Wireless Remote Control + 57" Tripod).

Video Editing Software, Mac Option   Final Cut Pro X (FCPX). Although slightly higher in price, a copy of FCPX, a high-performing video-editing software that handles the high-quality video from the best video cameras, would be a great choice. FCPX handles editing, audio, and green-screen effects better than any other Mac software on the market and is well worth the price.

Video Editing Software, PC Option Adobe Premiere Pro (APP). A professional-level digital video-editing program for PCs, APP is fast, with an easy interface, and handles editing, audio, and green-screen effects for a video format.

Lighting (and Green Screen) Video Studio Kit 1600 watt Complete Video Solution. The library investing this much time and effort into a SPOC should consider purchasing all-in-one set lighting. The set from TubeTape (http://www.tubetape.net/), which includes all the lighting equipment necessary for a video shoot, is a great example of the very basic for lighting. It also included a bonus green screen, which allows the instructor to walk a bit in front of images, and makes framing the MOOC much easier.

On the cheaper side, you could definitely use in-house lamps and lighting equipment, but you will have to buy green screen to use in the background for this SPOC. Green screens themselves can run as cheap as thirty-five dollars but will last for a long time with the proper care.

Platform Option 1 LearnDash. LearnDash is a supplemental WordPress MOOC platform add-on. It is easy to install, learn, and implement. If a library has already used, and is familiar with, the WordPress layout, the learning curve will be low for all staff, including the instructors. Again, LearnDash hosts SPOC videos, exercises, discussion board, quizzes, and other assessment all in one clean interface.

Platform Option 2 Google Groups and YouTube. If a library does not have a WordPress blog, or funding to support more technology purchases, you can easily use a combination of YouTube and Google Groups to host the video and provide a space for a discussion board. Google Groups can, with careful planning, also serve as a rudimentary assessment—mostly for short answers—but is nevertheless an excellent free option. Note that users must have a Google account in order to access the SPOC Google Group.

Q4.1. What Type of Formats Are Supported on Your Platform?

Option 1 LearnDash, via WordPress, allows the library to upload text, Word docs, pdf files, and embedded media from YouTube, Vimeo, or other video media sites.

Option 2   Google Groups and YouTube can handle the video posts, some of the assessment, and the required discussion board.

Q4.2. What Type of Assessments Are Supported on Your Platform?

Option 1   LearnDash supports almost every type of assessment including multiple choice, multiple answer, short answer, fill in the blank, discussion-board assignments, and more. The library SPOC will utilize a combination of multiple-choice quizzes, image quizzes, and discussion boards.

Option 2   Google Groups and YouTube will use short-answer assessment and the required discussion board.

Q5.1. What Is the Name of Your MOOC?

TrackRef SPOC

Q5.2. What Is the Duration of Your MOOC (Weeks)?

Three weeks.

Q5.3. What Is the Topic of Your MOOC?

Library staff development and training using the new TrackRef system.

Q6.1. What Is the Target Country, State, or Town for Your MOOC?

The LibraryX TrackRef SPOC is open to all library staff in the academic consortium. Those involved in reference will be most likely to benefit from the SPOC, but others may also be interested in the general information about new software being utilized for libraries.

Q6.2. What Is the Level of Education Necessary to Take Your MOOC?

No particular level required—all library staff members, regardless of an MLIS, are welcome.

Q7.1. What Are the Learning Objectives of the MOOC?

1. Obtain a basic comprehension of the features of the new Track-Ref software.
2. Utilize the new technology to simplify the creation of on-point library data.

Q7.2. What Competencies Will Participants Acquire in the MOOC?

1. Learn effective time management for reference questions.
2. Use reference data to inform other parts of the library's work (collection, acquisitions, etc.).

Q8.1. What Is the Structure of the MOOC?

Six modules (two modules per week).

Q8.2. What Format(s) Will You Utilize for Your MOOC Contents?

Videos, PowerPoint slides, quick LibGuides, and other media (as appropriate).

Q9.1. What Type of Weekly Assessment Will the MOOC Utilize?

Multiple-choice quizzes, image quizzes, and discussion boards.

Q9.2. What Type of Final Assessment Will the MOOC Utilize?

The final assessment could be a series of reference questions, which will be answered and recorded using the TrackRef live. Participants may receive follow-up questions to show their knowledge on gathering reference-question data from the system.

Q10.1. Will You Use Additional Media for Advertising, Promotion, Discussion, and So Forth?

The library will use its internal library listserv for promotional purposes.

Now that we have used the MOOC appraisal sheet to decide about some of our bigger planning concerns, let's move on to the basic content and structure.

Basic Elements of the TrackRef SPOC

1. Lectures—videos presented by the TrackRef SPOC instructors, later uploaded to YouTube after postprocessing.
2. In-lecture quizzes—simple multiple-choice questions appear midlecture, designed to aid the participant's pace and monitor

progress. These are not graded but a form of in-lecture assessment.

3. Weekly multiple-choice sets (one a week for weeks one through four)—basic quiz featuring multiple-choice questions.
4. Weekly video check-in—the instructor provides commentary to some of the previous week's TrackRef problems. Reemphasizes the learning outcome from that week.
5. Final exam—a series of reference questions, which will be answered and recorded using the TrackRef live. Participants may receive follow-up questions to show their knowledge on gathering reference-question data from the system.

Let's view each of these content categories for this class in a little more detail in the pre- and postproduction process.

Creating the SPOC Video Lecture in Preproduction

Here are some important pointers when filming using the proposed SPOC with basic green-screen technology. (Many of these tips would also apply to any MOOC video shoot as well.)

- Place the camera at the back of the room, positioning the camera so that it could zoom in on the instructor for a close-up shot, if necessary.
- The green screen should be set up behind the lecturer.
- For this shoot, and others that utilizes slides and or visual aids, you might consider a small podium with a laptop set up next to the instructor. This gives the instructor freedom to move about, if necessary, during the lecture.
- The audio can be recorded on a lapel mic or, if necessary, a mic set up near the podium.
- Keep the room well lit for the shoot, both by overhead lights and, if necessary, additional lighting that you can control (for example, the Video Studio Kit by TubeTape covered in chapter 3, which includes two professional-grade lights to light both the background and the instructor).

- Draw all the shades and curtains to keep out light beyond the room control (sometimes blankets and tape are useful for this task).

Green-screen Pointers

Using a green screen for the first time may seem like a daunting task, but it will really add to the professional look and feel of your SPOC. Take the time to make these pointers part of your preproduction setup and strategy. Getting it right the first time prevents the time, cost, and technical frustration of editing errors and mistakes in postproduction.

- Each instructor should avoid wearing clothes that are similar to whatever color is used in the background. For example, make sure you avoid greens, browns, and khaki for green-screen shoots and jeans and other blue clothes for blue-screen shoots. Always, no matter what color you use in the background of a MOOC, do not wear the same color as the green-screen background. Also, white clothing is difficult to light properly.
- Avoid clothes and props that are reflective. Sequins, sparkles, reflective night gear, and other reflective clothing are also best left out of the MOOC production.
- Check the shot to make sure the background of your image doesn't have anything that shouldn't be there: extension cords, papers, tape, etc.
- Keep the green screen as clean as possible, and stop people from walking on it unnecessarily.
- Use a regular camera to take reference shots for lighting, podium location, and screen location, just in case you need to reshoot or add to this SPOC production later. You want any additional shooting to be as uniform as possible.

Best Practices during SPOC Production

- For the equipment: Bring extra batteries, cables, memory, extension cords, tape, and light bulbs.
- For the instructors: Bring water, tissues/paper towels, paper, and pen.

- Create hand signals between the assistants behind the camera and the instructors just in case problems arise, such as battery failure, memory issues, or any other issue. With hand signals, production could still go on or be fixed, without interrupting the audio. For example, many cameras have a recording limit. If the camera was about to go over the limit, the assistant could hand signal the instructor, and adjustment could be made on the fly.
- Break the lectures into small segments (approximately seven to ten minutes). For example, the proposed TrackRef SPOC is made up of six modules, deployed over three weeks, so you may film even smaller segments and add them together later in postproduction. In the option where there is a wireless remote control at the instructor's podium, instructors can start or stop the filming at their own directive, which will make for a clean transition between topics.

Postproduction Recommended Process

This is our advanced SPOC project, so in this hypothetical we are using software in the postproduction process that can handle green-screen effects. Final Cut Pro X and Adobe Premiere Pro (both reviewed in chapter 3) allow a person to use a "chroma key" in your video footage without sending your clips to any other software program, such as After Effects. Keying with FCPX and APP is clear cut and effective. Here are some basic workflow recommendations for postproduction editing in our advanced SPOC.

1. Import. One of the first things to do after the video shooting is complete is to import the media into the video-editing system. Then you can sync up the audio from the mics with the main video. As noted in its review, FCPX does an excellent job of syncing audio and video. APP provides a method for synchronizing audio and video called Merge Clips. Syncing is critical in achieving good audio performance, as you move into other forms of postproduction.

2. Chroma-key green-screen effect. Next, using the chroma-keying program in your software, you can drop in the background on the green screen. In this case we have chosen a nice blue hue for the background when the instructor is talking to the SPOC partici-

pants. Note that this part of the editing process can take time, especially if you are just learning the program for the first time. However, later, as you become more comfortable with the software and editing process, you do not have to surrender as much time to still get a quality outcome. Some MOOC editors have recommended that if you have many smaller clips, it may be handy to create a "compound clip." Then you can make all the edits in the larger clip, rather than taking the time for each individual clip's editing process.

3. Further trim and edits. APP and FCPX allows you to trim up the clips for the smoothest transition. You can also eliminate any awkward pauses, misstatements, those occasional "ums" that come with lecturing, and other imperfections.

4. Add in the TrackRef PowerPoint slides. As we reviewed earlier, TrackRef gave us slides that we included in our screencast, as we were recording our video shot. You can now add the TrackRef PowerPoint slides as they appear in the video, using the synced audio/video from the shoot. These are imported from the screen-recording program that was running at the same time as the lecture. Then you have a chance to edit them as they are worked into the overall segment. Since the screencast may be at a different resolution than the instructor's lecture with the video camera, you might have to use APP or FCPX to frame or zoom in at certain segments, and on certain slides.

5. Add transitions, opening, and closing. You are nearly completed, so at this point you can add any of the video-editing program's featured transitions—from fade-out to screen wipes. The opening and closing should be uniform for each module of the SPOC, so creating them one time and adding them to the video should be simple.

6. Watch, edit, and repeat. Have a colleague take a look at the "final product," but be prepared to make changes based on feedback.

7. Export. Once the modules are ready to deploy, you can upload them into the library's YouTube account. These links will remain private, meaning no one can find them online without the private URLs assigned by YouTube. From here all it takes is a simple embed code to launch them in our SPOC platform site.

NOTES

1. Robert F. Mager, *Preparing Instructional Objectives*, Mager, 2nd ed. (Belmont, CA: David S. Lake, 1984).

2. Philip J. Guo, Juho Kim, and Rob Rubin, "How Video Production Affects Student Engagement: An Empirical Study of MOOC Videos," in Learning at Scale 2014, Proceedings of the First ACM Conference on Learning at Scale Conference, March 4–5, Atlanta, 41–50, http://dl.acm.org/.

3. Philip Guo, "How MOOC Video Production Affects Student Engagement," edX, March 12, 2014, accessed December 20, 2014, https://www.edx.org/.

6

TIPS AND TRICKS

In this chapter, we will very briefly examine some sage advice from librarians who have been involved with massive open online courses (MOOCs). From guiding MOOC faculty to open resources to getting the right department involved in a MOOC, there are some tips and tricks that librarians working with MOOCs will find helpful.

LIBRARIES AND MOOCS: MEET FIRST, MEET OFTEN

It almost goes without saying that being involved with MOOCs at the "ground floor" or at the very beginning of a MOOC is an essential element for any successful collaboration. As we have seen, MOOCs, at least the most successful ones, clearly use more than just a talking faculty member to make their teaching available online. The use of outstanding multimedia course materials—pictures, text, film, 3-D objects, databases, and more—is what separates the average MOOC from the engaging MOOC. And more often than not, who has the mission to collect, preserve, and provide access to these learning materials? Librarians.

Therefore, it is critical that the library be front and center at any organization that plans on launching a MOOC. This could be as simple as having the library staff create and launch the MOOC (as in the "Copyright for Librarians" MOOC at Duke), or having the library support the experts creating the class, whether at a public library (BostonX) or an academic library (UPenn supporting faculty teaching Coursera courses).

As we have outlined in previous chapters, the library can play a critical role in copyright assessment, syllabus support, teaching, open access, research, and more. The policy trick is to clearly outline all of the potential sources for collaboration between the library and the MOOC.

OPEN ACCESS AND OPPORTUNITIES

You can't learn from a resource you don't have access to.—Will Cross, director, Copyright and Digital Scholarship Center [1]

Open access was defined at the Budapest Open Access Initiative in 2002 as "free availability on the public Internet, permitting any users to read, download, copy, distribute, print, search, or link to the full texts of these articles, crawl them for indexing, pass them as data to software, or use them for any other lawful purpose, without financial, legal, or technical barriers other than those inseparable from gaining access to the internet itself." By its very definition, we can see how using open-access materials would be of enormous value to libraries working with MOOCs. There are very few problems with licensing, rights, access, or cost when using open-access materials. Imagine all the work that could be saved by using materials that can be freely shared, modified, adapted, or revised to serve the MOOC's pedagogical purpose.

Librarians, strong leaders in the open-access movement, are typically in the best position to point out the wealth of open-access material available—through research guides, classroom instruction, catalog integration, and more. Many librarians working with MOOCs are compelled by the mission and vision of MOOCs to make readings, textbooks, and other materials free to access for all participants worldwide. Requiring a textbook for purchase is common for on-ground courses, but not typically for MOOCs.

Many scholarly communications librarians, copyright librarians, and open-access librarians have acknowledged that the MOOC revolution can be a great catalyst for further action toward understanding and realizing the true potential for open educational materials. Kevin Smith, at Duke University, shared this brief story about open-access materials and MOOCs:

> One story will illustrate this growing interest in open access. A faculty member who was recently preparing to teach his first MOOC wanted his students to be able to read several of his own articles. When we asked his publisher for permission on his behalf, it was denied. A rude awakening for our professor, but also an opportunity to talk about open access. As it turned out, all of the articles were published in journals that allowed the author to deposit his final manuscripts, and this author had them all. So we uploaded those post-prints, and he had persistent, no-cost links to provide to the 80,000 students who were registered for his course. An eye-opener for the author, a missed opportunity for the publisher, and a small triumph for our OA repository. Enough of a triumph that this professor has begun asking colleagues if they could deposit post-prints of their own articles in the repositories at their institutions so that he can use those for his MOOC students as well.[2]

Here are some of the most common, most accessible, and most thorough links and sites for finding and using open-access materials for a MOOC or other open educational resource:

Open-Access Books

- HathiTrust Digital Library (http://www.hathitrust.org/)
- Internet Archive (IA) Ebook and Texts (http://archive.org/details/texts)
- Directory of Open Access Books (DOAB) (http://www.doabooks.org/)

Open-Access Textbooks

- University of Minnesota Open Textbook Catalog (https://open.umn.edu/opentextbooks/)

Open-Access Journals and Articles

- Directory of Open Access Journals (http://www.doaj.org/)

- CreativeCommons attribution licensed journals (http://en.wikipedia.org/)
- PubMed Central (http://www.ncbi.nlm.nih.gov/pmc/)
- Proceedings of the National Academy of Sciences (PNAS) (http://www.pnas.org/)
- Public Library of Science (PLOS) (http://www.plos.org/)

Other Open-Access Media

Carli Spina, emerging technologies and research librarian at Harvard Law School Library, has developed a basic LibGuide for MOOC communities to help them find open access (OA), Creative Commons, public domain, and other freely licensed media. Titled "Finding Public Domain and Creative Commons Media," this frequently cited guide is one of the best sources available for finding open material. The guide is divided into the database resources most sought after by MOOCs: audio, video, and images. Each database is annotated by Spina, who denotes the true "openness" of each resource. She also advises users to use different search methodologies for particular databases in order to find content in the public domain or freely licensed.

Spina consistently updates her LibGuide, reflecting the changing open-access policies at museums, archives, libraries, and other content-heavy organizations. If a resource is free of rights and available on the web, Spina will have most likely included it in her database guide. Have a look at her guide, "Finding Public Domain and Creative Commons Media," on the Harvard Law School Library website (http://guides.library.harvard.edu/), and you will probably bookmark it for your open-access MOOC work.

INVOLVING THE RIGHT LIBRARY DEPARTMENT

A question that is often asked when looking at the landscape of MOOCs is, Where are the librarians? The future of the role of librarians involved in MOOCs is unclear. While this book has reviewed the many ways in which MOOCs can enhance a library's mission, knowledge, and connection within a community, others note that librarians may not be required in the MOOC world. According to Gillian S. Gremmels, the "bleakest outlook for academic libraries in the MOOC environment may be that no one needs us."[3] MOOCs typically are skills-based, job-related courses that last only four to eight weeks. In classes such as these, traditional librarian involvement may well be unnecessary. It is up to each library, however, to refute that concept. Looking across the landscape of unique and tech-savvy departments within libraries, one can see a wealth of potential roles for various library departments.

Which library department is best suited to support a MOOC? Well, a lot depends on the MOOC. In certain circumstances, librarians can expect to take on roles that are similar to those they have within traditional courses. For example, the University of Florida (UF) Levin College of Law's "Global Student's Introduction to U.S. Law," offered through Coursera, features six UF Law professors and two librarians. This eight-week course was the first MOOC offered by the Levin College of Law, and it was expected that librarians from both the research and the instruction departments would design legal research classes with corresponding quizzes, as they would for the on-ground version of the class. Involving the Research & Instruction department in the beginning of the course opened up the idea that other library departments might be useful for the MOOC production.

Advanced humanities classes, covering topics such as Greek paintings or the music of Mozart, often require access to rare and archived materials. What better position could the special collections and archive librarians be in to make the wealth of their department's treasure available to the MOOC audience around the world? This would involve both preservation specialists and, more than likely, some aspect of any library digitization department. What about a class on public health and medicine? Wouldn't the library's subject specialist be in the best position to help faculty identify and locate alternative materials, such as National Institutes of Health (NIH)–funded reports, that are free of copyright constraints because they are made available under either Creative Commons or open-access licenses? And in the last example, what about a library-focused class, as we have examined in our hypothetical MOOC projects? Here the answer is obvious: the librarians should be teaching the class. Again, it's about involving the experts on a particular topic, or a particular function, and the librarian with that expertise is in the best position to provide the support necessary.

Of the varied MOOC classes where the library played a role, the following library departments or library individuals were explicitly mentioned as a critical part of a MOOC's success:

- Reference and research services departments
- Teaching, learning, and curriculum departments
- Preservation services departments
- Special collections and archives departments
- Metadata and cataloging librarians
- Digital humanities librarians
- Digital library systems and services
- Music, art, film, law, business, design, religion, education, and so forth, librarians
- Copyright/licensing librarians
- Open-access librarians

Librarian inclusion in MOOCs and MOOC support teams is a foregone conclusion in many environments. At larger MOOC institutions, such as Coursera or edX, many library departments play leading roles in assisting instructors. This trend is bound to continue and perhaps even create new MOOC library positions that mix the library profession's expertise in information literacy, instructional design, and online learning pedagogy—all rolled into one.

NOTES

1. From Twitter, November 19, 2014, RT @CharlotteRock "You Can't Learn from a Resource You Don't Have Access to." —Will Cross, NCSU #LibOER #opened14.

2. Kevin Smith, "The O in MOOC," Scholarly Communications@Duke, April 11, 2013, http://blogs.library.duke.edu/.

3. Gillian S. Gremmels, "Staffing Trends in College and University Libraries," *Reference Services Review* 41, no. 2 (2013): 233–52, http://dx.doi.org/.

7

FUTURE TRENDS

Since their inception, massive open online courses (MOOCs) have been heralded both as the future of higher education and as the educational equivalent of "junk food." Regardless, they appear to be here to stay, as more institutions are investing the time and resources to create MOOC experiences. In this chapter, we review some of the future developments involving both libraries and MOOCs.

To that end, the near future looks bright for both content creators and learners. What has started with toe-dipping on the part of public libraries and K–12 schools into the MOOC environment will likely become a more entrenched effort as these early experiences are studied and refined. One size does not fit all, and as much as academic institutions have spun off SPOCs (small private online courses) from MOOCs, public libraries and K–12 can be expected to leverage the technology and scope of MOOCs to innovative ends.

Another MOOC front ripe for change, which will require a significant investment in institutional resources, is the development of robust in-house content delivery systems. Currently, many MOOCs rely on third-party vendors (e.g., YouTube or Canvas Network) for course delivery. Institutions cede a great deal of the control of their content to these companies. By creating alternative, internal systems (like Stanford's Class2Go), institutions would assume less risk and have greater autonomy over the entire MOOC life cycle. Undertaking such an effort would likely be a cost-prohibitive effort for a smaller institution, but if a large institution were to take leadership on developing a stable, extensible, open-source alternative to said third-party tools, then the larger open-education community would benefit.

Similarly, there is room for greater collaboration between MOOC creators and beyond. While MOOC content is "open," the development, delivery, and storage are mostly siloed by institution and content provider. Libraries have long partnered on consortial agreements for resources; applying this similar behavior in the MOOC environment would help prevent duplication of effort and resources, and expand the reach of each individual content creator. Collaboration within an institution, which is essential to the successful development and delivery of a MOOC, would benefit by extending to public libraries, museums, and other cultural institutions, government organizations, and more. Such an effort would take coordination and initial investment to ramp up successfully, but once in place, this distributed network of resources would be mutually beneficial to all partners.

WHAT'S ON THE HORIZON FOR MOOCS AND LIBRARIES?

The role of libraries in MOOC development, which is rooted in collaboration, is one of great potential. While MOOCs are somewhat of a moving target, they present a unique opportunity for libraries to add expertise and value both to internal stakeholders and to the global community of MOOC participants.

At the start of the MOOC life cycle, librarians are critical team members in course development. From working with faculty on finding appropriate resources to scaffolding courses and providing copyright-related support, librarians already often serve as thought partners in the early stages of MOOC content creation. By advocating for extending their role to serve as a stronger presence within the course, librarians could add even greater value as co-instructors or embed themselves within the class to provide learners with more personalized, guided support. Doing so could potentially help retention rates and address pedagogy gaps that some critics of MOOCs cite.

Another opportunity for librarians is in creating learner-side services. As much as embedding librarians in every course could be beneficial, a similarly positive but less resource-intensive step would be to develop MOOC-specific research guides and partner with faculty on creating open educational resources (OERs). Librarians have the subject knowledge and familiarity with open-access resources to steer MOOC learners, who likely have limited access to licensed products and to sound, open-access scholarship. Leading participants to such content could also help retention rates and give the participants higher-level information literacy exposure. As well, OER content could certainly be repurposed for a faculty member's face-to-face teaching. Learners' usage could also be tracked, and the resulting data could be used to inform the development and improvement of future resources.

Librarians also have the opportunity to serve a critical function at the end of a MOOC's life cycle. Libraries are digitizing content for use in MOOCs and preserving MOOCs at their close. This is largely a siloed activity, as mentioned above. A great challenge for librarians would be to not only categorize and store this data but also advocate opening and sharing this data. This would require a coordinated effort to ensure all Internet protocol (IP) and technical issues are addressed properly, but the payoff would be tenfold. Much as creating a shared technical infrastructure for content delivery would be beneficial, so too would be the creation of a shared database of resources, content, and metadata upon which MOOC creators and others could draw.

MOOC RESEARCH

There is no dearth of data about MOOCs. Number reports have detailed information gleaned about course participants—from age and education level to participation rate. While this has resulted in a lot of numbers, there is the vague sense that we may not be asking the right questions of the data that we have and that we may not yet be collecting complete and sufficient data.

There is any number of questions related to MOOCs and their "success" that have yet to be properly addressed and solved: Why is retention rate so low? What supports can be implemented to improve student participation? Are the learners that are participating gaining the competencies the course aims to deliver? How are they using the information that is presented to them? How is student work assessed? Are the assessments used asking the right questions? If not, how should and can the course content and underlying pedagogy be shifted to have greater impact? How can that be measured? How are learners using third-party material in their course work, and are they doing so ethically? How can this data be digested and used to inform face-to-face teaching and learning? The list goes on.

What is the solution? Collect more comprehensive, deep data, and ask more questions. And it is critical that librarians participate in such assessment. By helping to hone the right questions, particularly related to information literacy, research support, and third-party resources, the library will be in the unique position to help improve MOOC experiences for future learners by filling gaps, shoring up pitfalls, and smoothing rough edges. Again, this information can be used to shape and improve online experiences for on-campus students.

Using data to hone services will help create a feedback loop that can direct and improve the shape of MOOCs to come, helping them to become powerful change agents both to the learners and to the participating faculty, librarians, and institutions, who may leverage this information to improve and innovate teaching and learning in a holistic manner.

RECOMMENDED READING

ONLINE PEDAGOGY

Brown University, School of Professional Studies. 2015. "Best Practices for Teaching Online." http://www.brown.edu/.

Colorado State University, Institute of Learning and Teaching. 2015. "Best Practices in Course Design: A Teaching Guide." http://teaching.colostate.edu/.

———. 2015. "Suggested Course Development Best Practices." http://teaching.colostate.edu/.

Hill, Christopher, ed. 2015. "10 Principles of Effective Online Teaching: Best Practices in Distance Education." Faculty Focus Special Report. Madison, WI: Magna. https://www.mnsu.edu/.

Holsombach-Ebner, Cinda. 2013. "Assurance in Large Scale Online Course Production." *Online Journal of Distance Learning Administration* 16, no. 2. http://www.westga.edu/.

Kelly, Rob. 2012. "Practical Advice for Going from Face to Face to Online Teaching." Faculty Focus, Online Education. February 9. http://www.facultyfocus.com/.

Oregon State University, Ecampus. 2015. "Overview of Best Practices for Online Course Design." http://ecampus.oregonstate.edu/.

Parscal, Tina, and Deborah Riemer. 2010. "Assuring Quality in Large-Scale Online Course Development." *Online Journal of Distance Learning Administration* 13, no. 2. http://www.westga.edu/.

Stevens, Karl B. 2013. "Contributing Factors to a Successful Online Course Development Process." *Journal of Continuing Higher Education* 61, no. 1: 2–11. http://dx.doi.org/.

University of Las Vegas Nevada, Office of Academic Affairs. 2015. "Best Practices for Teaching Online." https://online.unlv.edu/.

Vanderbilt University, Center for Teaching. 2015. "Coursera Resource Guide." http://cft.vanderbilt.edu/.

MOOCS 101

Christensen, Gayle, Andrew Steinmetz, Brandon Alcorn, Amy Bennett, Deirdre Woods, and Ezekiel J. Emanuel. 2013. "The MOOC Phenomenon: Who Takes Massive Open Online Courses and Why?" SSRN, November 6. http://dx.doi.org/.

Creed-Dikeogu, Gloria, and Carolyn Clark. 2013. "Are You MOOC-ing Yet? A Review for Academic Libraries." *Kansas Library Association College and University Libraries Section Proceedings* 3, no. 1: 5. http://dx.doi.org/.

EDUCAUSE Learning Initiative. 2011. "7 Things You Should Know about MOOCS." November. http://www.educause.edu/.

———. 2013. "7 Things You Should Know about MOOCS II." June. http://www.educause.edu/.

Littlejohn, Allison. 2013. "Understanding Massive Open Online Courses." EdTech Notes, Commonwealth Educational Media Centre for Asia. http://cemca.org.in/.

Wright, Forrest. 2013. "What Do Librarians Need to Know about MOOCs?" *D-Lib Magazine* 19, nos. 3/4. http://dx.doi.org/.

Wu, Kerry. 2013. "Academic Libraries in the Age of MOOCs." *Reference Services Review* 41, no. 3: 576–87. http://dx.doi.org/.

MOOCS, COPYRIGHT, AND FAIR USE

Barnes, Cameron. 2013. "MOOCs: The Challenges for Academic Librarians." *Australian Academic and Research Libraries* 44, no. 3: 163–75. http://dx.doi.org/.

Brennan Croft, Janet. 2013. "MOOCS and Copyright: Maybe Not Fifty Shades of Gray, But Close." *Oklahoma Librarian* 63, no. 2. http://www.oklibrarian.org/with.

Calter, Mariellen. 2013. "MOOCs and the Library: Engaging with Evolving Pedagogy." IFLA World Library and Information Congress, 79th IFLA General Conference and Assembly, August 17–23, Singapore. http://library.ifla.org/.

Cheverie, Joan. 2013. "Copyright Challenges in a MOOC Environment." EDUCAUSE Brief. July 29. http://www.educause.edu/.

Dames, K. Matthew. 2013. "Copyright Norms Clash with MOOCs." *Information Today* 30, no. 9: 24. http://connection.ebscohost.com/.

Fowler, Lauren, and Kevin Smith. 2013. "Drawing the Blueprint as We Build: Setting Up a Library-Based Copyright and Permissions Service for MOOCs." *D-Lib Magazine* 19, nos. 7/8. http://dx.doi.org/.

Fusch, Daniel. 2013. "How Will MOOCs Affect Fair Use and Copyright Compliance?" Academic Impressions, Higher Ed Impact. January 11. http://www.academicimpressions.com/.

University of North Carolina at Chapel Hill, Scholarly Communications Office. 2013. "Guidelines for Using Copyrighted Material in Coursera MOOCs." http://library.unc.edu/
.

MOOCS AND LIBRARY SERVICES

American Library Association, Association for Library Collections and Technical Services. 2013–2014. ALCTS Webinar Series: Libraries and MOOCs. December 11–June 4. http://www.ala.org/.

Becker, Bernd W. 2013. "Connecting MOOCs and Library Services." *Behavioral and Social Sciences Librarian* 32, no. 2: 135–38. http://dx.doi.org/.

Bond, Paul (contributor), and Faye Leibowitz (column ed.). 2013. "MOOCs and Serials." *Serials Review* 39, no. 4: 258–60. http://dx.doi.org/.

Butler, Brandon. 2012. "Massive Open Online Courses: Legal and Policy Issues for Research Libraries." Association of Research Libraries, Issue Brief, October 22. http://www.arl.org/.

Chant, Ian. 2013. "Opening Up: Next Steps for MOOCs and Libraries." *Library Journal, Academic Newswire*, December 10. http://lj.libraryjournal.com/.

Dartmouth College. 2015. "MOOCs and More! Articles on Libraries and MOOCs." Library Research Guides. http://researchguides.dartmouth.edu/.

Gore, Hannah. 2014. "Massive Open Online Courses (MOOCs) and Their Impact on Academic Library Services: Exploring the Issues and Challenges." *New Review of Academic Librarianship* 20, no. 1: 4–28. http://dx.doi.org/.

Mahraj, Katy. 2012. "Using Information Expertise to Enhance Massive Open Online Courses." *Public Services Quarterly* 8, no. 4: 359–68. http://dx.doi.org/.

Massis, Bruce E. 2013. "MOOCs and the Library." *New Library World* 114, nos. 5/6: 267–70. http://dx.doi.org/.

OCLC. 2013. "MOOCs and Libraries: Massive Opportunity or Overwhelming Challenge?" Presentation by OCLC Research and the University of Pennsylvania Libraries, March 18–19, Philadelphia.

Pennsylvania State University. 2014. "Penn State Libraries Create Research Guides for MOOCs." *Penn State News*, September 26. http://news.psu.edu/.

Proffitt, Merrilee. 2013. "MOOCs and Libraries: An Overview of the Landscape, and How Libraries Can Serve the 'Inside Out' Classroom." European Libraries Automation Group (ELAG), May 28–31, Ghent, Belgium. http://elag2013.org/.

Sampson, Sara, and Leslie Anne Street. "The Promise and Perils of Massive Open Online Courses: MOOCs and the Role of Law Librarians." *AALL Spectrum* 18, no. 4: 9–11. http://connection.ebscohost.com/.

Schwartz, Meredith. 2013. "Massive Open Opportunity: Supporting MOOCs in Public and Academic Libraries." *Library Journal, Academic Newswire*, May 10. http://lj.libraryjournal.com/.

Wu, Kerry. 2013. "Academic Libraries in the Age of MOOCs." *Reference Services Review* 41, no. 3: 576–87. http://dx.doi.org/.

FUTURE FOR MOOCS + LIBRARIES

Dasarathy, Balakrishnan, Kevin Sullivan, Douglas C. Schmidt, Douglas H. Fisher, and Adam Porter. 2014. "The Past, Present, and Future of MOOCs and Their Relevance to Software Engineering." In Proceedings of the on Future of Software Engineering (FOSE). May 31–June 7, New York. ACM Digital Library, 212–24. doi:10.1145/2593882.2593897.

Fischer, Gerhard. 2014. "Beyond Hype and Underestimation: Identifying Research Challenges for the Future of MOOCs." *Distance Education* 35, no. 2: 149–58. doi:10.1080/01587919.2014.920752.

Harman, Keith, and Alex Koohang. 2013. "MOOC 2050: A Futuristic Tour." *Issues in Information Systems* 14, no. 2: 346–52.

Kroski, Ellyssa. 2013. "The Future of MOOCs." Open Education Database. http://oedb.org/.

O'Brien, Lynne. 2012. "Massive Open Online Courses as Drivers for Change." CNI Fall 2012 Membership Meeting, December 10–11, Washington, DC. http://cit.duke.edu/.

MOOCS + RESEARCH

Baggaley, Jon. "MOOCs: Digesting the Facts." *Distance Education* 35, no. 2: 159–63. doi:10.1080/01587919.2014.919710.

Ball, M. "MOOC Pedagogy: Gleaning Good Practice from Existing MOOCs." *Journal of Online Learning and Teaching* 10: 44–56.

Breslow, Lori, David E. Pritchard, Jennifer DeBoer, Glenda S. Stump, Andrew D. Ho, and Daniel T. Seaton. 2013. "Studying Learning in the Worldwide Classroom: Research into EdX's First MOOC." *Research and Practice in Assessment* 8 (Summer). http://www.rpajournal.com/.

Colvin, Kimberly F., John Champaign, Alwina Liu, Qian Zhou, Colin Fredericks, and David E. Pritchard. 2014. "Learning in an Introductory Physics MOOC: All Cohorts Learn Equally, Including an On-Campus Class." *International Review of Research in Open and Distributed Learning* 15, no. 4. http://www.irrodl.org/with.

Cress, Ulrike, and Carlos Delgado Kloos, eds. 2014. Proceedings of the European MOOC Stakeholder Summit 2014: EMOOCs 2014, European MOOCs Stakeholder Summit, February 10–12, Open Education Europa. http://www.emoocs2014.eu/.

Distance Education. 2014. Special Issue: *MOOCs: Emerging Research* 35, no. 2: 141–62.

Guo, Philip J., Juho Kim, and Rob Rubin. 2014. "How Video Production Affects Student Engagement: An Empirical Study of MOOC Videos." In Learning at Scale 2014, Proceedings of the First ACM Conference on Learning at Scale Conference, March 4–5, Atlanta, 41–50. http://dl.acm.org/.

Harvard University, HarvardX. 2015. "HarvardX Working Papers." http://harvardx.harvard.edu/.

Ho, Andrew D., Justin Reich, Sergiy Nesterko, Daniel T. Seaton, Tommy Mullaney, Jim Waldo, and Isaac Chuang. 2014. "HarvardX and MITx: The First Year of Open Online Courses." HarvardX Working Paper No. 1. http://harvardx.harvard.edu/.

Jordan, Katy. 2014. "Initial Trends in Enrolment and Completion of Massive Open Online Courses." *International Review of Research in Open and Distributed Learning* 15, no. 1. http://www.irrodl.org/with.

Khalil, Hanan, and Martin Ebner. 2013. "'How Satisfied Are You with Your MOOC?' A Research Study on Interaction in Huge Online Courses." In Proceedings of World Conference on Educational Multimedia, Hypermedia and Telecommunications, ed. Jan Herrington et al., Association for the Advancement of Computing in Education (AACE), June 24, Chesapeake, VA, 830–39.

Means, Barbara, Yukie Toyama, Robert Murphy, Marianne Bakia, and Karla Jones. 2009. "Evaluation of Evidence-Based Practices in Online Learning: A Meta-Analysis and Review of Online Learning Studies." U.S. Department of Education Office of Planning, Evaluation, and Policy Development Policy and Program Studies Service. http://www2.ed.gov/.

MOOC Research. 2015. MOOC Research Initiative (MRI) Grantee Reports. http://www.moocresearch.com/reports.

Perna, Laura, Alan Ruby, Robert Boruch, Nicole Wang, Janie Scull, Chad Evans, and Seher Ahmad. 2013. "The Life Cycle of a Million MOOC Users." University of Pennsylvania, MOOC Research Initiative Conference, December 5–6. Arlington, TX. http://www.gse.upenn.edu/.

Pritchard, Sarah M. 2013. "MOOCs: An Opportunity for Innovation and Research." *Libraries and the Academy* 13, no. 2: 127–29. doi:10.1353/pla.2013.0015.

Sandeen, Cathy. 2013. "Integrating MOOCS into Traditional Higher Education: The Emerging 'MOOC 3.0' Era." *Change: The Magazine of Higher Learning* 45, no. 6: 34–39. doi:10.1080/00091383.2013.842103.

Stein, Kat. 2013. "Penn GSE Study Shows MOOCs Have Relatively Few Active Users, with Only a Few Persisting to Course End." Pennsylvania State University Graduate School of Education Press Room, December 5. http://www.gse.upenn.edu/.

Yousef, A. M. F., M. A. Chatti, U. Schroeder, and M. Wosnitza. 2014. "What Drives a Successful MOOC? An Empirical Examination of Criteria to Assure Design Quality of MOOCs." 2014 IEEE 14th International Conference on Advanced Learning Technologies (ICALT), July 7–10, Athens, Greece, 44–48. doi:10.1109/ICALT.2014.23.

INDEX

ABOUT THE AUTHOR

Kyle K. Courtney is the copyright advisor and program manager at Harvard University, working out of the Office for Scholarly Communication. He works closely with Harvard Library to establish a culture of shared understanding of copyright issues among Harvard staff, faculty, and students. His work at Harvard also includes a role as the copyright and information policy advisor for Harvard's MOOC, HarvardX. He serves on several advisory committees that deal with libraries and MOOCs, including working with ACRL, ALA, and edX. He runs a copyright-law consulting practice for libraries, higher education institutions, nonprofit groups, and specialized archives. Before joining Harvard University, Kyle worked at Harvard Law School as the manager of Faculty Research and Scholarship.

Kyle also currently maintains a dual appointment at Northeastern University: as an affiliated scholar for the Program on Human Rights and the Global Economy (PHRGE) at the School of Law; and teaching "Cyberlaw: Privacy, Ethics, and Digital Rights" for the interdisciplinary Information Assurance program at the College of Computer and Information Science. He holds a JD with distinction in intellectual property law and an MSLIS. He is a published author and nationally recognized speaker on the topic of libraries and copyright. Kyle is on Twitter: @KyleKCourtney, and his main blog is at http://kylecourtney.com/.